# How to be A Good TEACHER

Rupal Jain

PUSTAK MAHAL®

*Publishers*
**Pustak Mahal**

***Administrative office and sale centre***

J-3/16 , Daryaganj, New Delhi-110002
☎ 011-23276539, 23272783, 23272784, 23260518
*E-mail:* info@pustakmahal.com • *Website:* www.pustakmahal.com

***Branches***
**Bengaluru:** ☎ 080-22234025, 40912845
*E-mail*: pustakmahalblr@gmail.com
**Mumbai:** ☎ 022-22010941, 22053387
*E-mail*: unicornbooksmumbai@gmail.com



ISBN 978-81-223-1396-3

**Edition 2020**



***Printed at :*** Unique Color Carton, Delhi

To

My Parents,

Mrs. Madhu Parekh and Mr. Hemant Parekh

Who are the real teacher's of my life.

# Teachers

The teacher's place in society is of vital importance. He acts as the pivot for the transmission of intellectual traditions and technical skills from generation to generation and helps to keep the lamp of civilization burning.

– Dr. S. Radhakrishnan

When you ask school going kids as to what will they like to become when they grow up, many of them will have a common answer i.e. Teacher. Teaching has always been considered as one of the noblest profession by mankind. Formal teaching is mainly done by qualified professionals, who in turn are paid for their service. In many countries, teachers require formal education and qualification to become a professional teacher. Any institute without a good teacher is just like a fish without water or body without soul. I know you all have adequate knowledge in your subjects. So, in this book, I have not focussed on subject related knowledge. What will be discussed instead are a few interpersonal qualities that a good teacher needs, in order to be the best. These basic qualities are as follows.

- Teaching ability
- Endurance
- Aptitude
- Willingness to share knowledge
- Humanity
- Pleasant nature
- Crisis management

We often consider a teacher's responsibility to be restricted only till the classroom. However, a teacher has a proficient role to play beyond classroom teaching. Outside the classroom, a teacher performs various functions like assisting the institute in curricular, extracurricular and co-curricular activities. A teacher has to analyze his/her personal skills, depth of knowledge, student's background, their requirements, the institute's expectations, current trends and techniques and syllabus decided by the board, before crafting the teaching plan. The Secondary Education Commission observes that every teacher and educationist of experience knows that even the best curriculum and the perfect syllabus remain dead unless enlivened by the right method of teaching and the right kind of teachers.

I have conducted a research to find out the problems faced by most teachers. The major challenges they face are as follows.

- Poor discipline among students.
- Low motivation levels as they study only for grades or marks.
- Lack of encouragement from parents.
- High absenteeism due to most of them joining coaching classes or private tuition.
- Lack of basic communication skills.
- Pessimistic attitude.
- Lack of personal aspirations, goals or objectives.

Successful teachers spend additional time and efforts in continuously communicating with the students, and encouraging their participation and feedback. They nurture, educate and guide their students to assist them in building their future and contribute to the betterment of the nation and become a good citizen.

guru brahma gurur vishnu
guru devo maheshwaraha
guru saakshat para brahma
tasmai sri-gurave namaha

गुरुर्ब्रह्मा गुरुर्विष्णुः गुरुर्देवो महेश्वरः।
गुरुरेव परंब्रह्म तस्मै श्रीगुरवे नमः।।

This Indian prayer states that the teacher is Brahma, the creator, Vishnu, the protector and Maheshwar, the controller. He is the entire universe personified, salutations to him.

Along with parents, teachers are equally responsible for instilling values, positive attitude and good manners in children.

Children are considered to be the future of any country. A child's mind is like clay. Just as clay can be given any desired shape, students can be moulded by their teachers and parents.

In our lives, we find different types of teachers, each with a unique set of strengths and limitations. But we remember only few of them throughout our lives. Have we ever analyzed why we consider some teachers better than others? What unique traits differentiate them? Why students' constantly encounter problems with only a few teachers? Why students neglect some teachers, but look up to a few. Researchers have revealed a direct correlation between a teacher's zeal and a student's learning and understanding. Teachers who are pleasant, gracious and compassionate always receive more respect in and outside the classroom.

A positively motivating teacher can easily transfer their enthusiasm to the students. They not only teach what they are expected to, but frequently try to explore new techniques to make the session more interactive, participative, enthusiastic and interesting. Well informed, intellectual, trained and highly professional teachers can easily transform a dull student into an interested one. They play a vital role in any student's life. They have to accept and appreciate the fact that each student comes from a different background and culture. They hold different beliefs and conventions. Therefore they will react in different ways.

Henry Von Dyke has said about teachers and teaching, "Ah! There you have the worst paid and the best rewarded of vocations. Do not enter it unless you love it. For the vast majority of men and women, it has no promise of wealth and fame, but they, to whom it is dear for its own sake are among the nobility of mankind. I sing the praise of the unknown teacher, king of himself and leader of the mankind".

In this 21st century, in addition to studies, parents expect their child to be the best in every field. So, the duties of teachers are expanding and teaching has become a very multi-faceted and challenging task. Good teachers should aim at:-

- Fostering obedience and discipline among students.
- Avoiding corporal punishment to teach students a lesson.
- Assisting their students in deciding their personal goals (beyond educational perspective) and intellectual objective (academic target).
- Demonstrating zest for their institute, students, subject, colleagues, teaching and learning something new every day. Sometimes, the information offered in the text books is obsolete, but a good teacher remains abreast with the latest information and shares it with their students. Rabindranath Tagore once said that a teacher can never truly teach unless he is still learning himself. A lamp can never light another lamp unless it continues to burn in its own flame. The teacher who has come to the end of his subject, who has no living traffic with his knowledge, but merely repeats his lessons to his students, can only load their minds. He cannot engage them.
- Encouraging students to participate in extracurricular activities is essential as "all work and no play makes jack a dull boy".
- Being a role model for their students. Not only by their speech, but also by their actions. Many times, students try to imitate their teachers. Their way of communication, their body language, teaching techniques do have a great impact on students. For many students their teachers are their friend, philosopher, guide, information reservoir, catalyst and motivator. According to me, they are genuine craftsmen of any country. A teacher's appearance, mannerism, enthusiasm, nature, values, confidence, self discipline, dedication, devotion, knowledge, creativity, intelligence, punctuality, attitude, professional competency, determination, loyalty, generosity, coordination as well as educational achievements play a vital role in stimulating students. For this, it is very vital for all teachers to love their job.

- Facilitating students with mental, emotional and physical stability and thereby imparting excellent education to all the students.
- Nurturing them without any discrimination based on caste, creed, gender, religion, age or race.
- Developing high moral and ethical values among students.
- Encouraging patriotic feeling among students.
- Encouraging them to "think global and act local".
- Developing rational thinking and questioning attitude among students.
- Inspiring students to overcome all problems in life with courage and perseverence.
- Assisting the institute in designing a curriculum that balances the curricular and extra curricular activities. This in turn reflects in the personal and academic growth of every student.
- Knowing when and how to lighted up or intensify the mood in the classroom.
- Encouraging students to participate in the session and ask questions, as some students are very shy and afraid of asking questions, especially to their teachers. An interactive and participative environment can stimulate students to ask for guidance or help directly from teachers rather than approaching their classmates. As Swami Vivekananda rightly believed, the true teacher is he who can immediately come down to the level of the student, transfer his soul to the student, see through and understand through his mind.

For ease in reading, I have divided this book into various chapters. A teacher has to play multifaceted roles within the institute. So, each chapter refers to a technique in which you can enhance your skills and competencies with a social group. Happy reading!

# Contents

# 15 Ways to Motivate Students

## Canon 1: Give prompt, regular and affirmative feedback

*"A gem is not polished without rubbing, nor a man perfected without trials"*
*– Chinese proverb.*

Feedback is the connecting link between a student's performance and the teacher's expectation. In other words, it is teacher's evaluation of the student's performance. If you are happy with someone's performance, appreciate it. Admiration is free of cost and gives instant results. On the other hand, criticism can be hurtful. So, good communication is very important to convey your message. Think before you speak. While giving feedback, show some amount of consideration towards the students to understand the students' point of view as well. You should aim to motivate students only to perform better.

Appreciation is the prime motivator to all students. Commend their efforts; even the minutest. Give credit to the students when they deserve it. Keep in mind the golden rule that a good teacher must appreciate publicly, but criticize personally. A good teacher remains cool and calm in unfavourable situations as well.

This can be better explained in the words of Gary R. Casselman & Timothy C. Daughtry.

"Criticism is driven by the frustration and fears of the giver, not from the needs of the recipient. The underlying assumption is that the recipient somehow "should know better" and needs to be set straight.

The message implied is that the recipient's intentions are questionable, that there is something wrong with the recipient that the giver of criticism knows how to fix. In criticism, the problem is all in the recipient.

In contrast, feedback has an air of concern, respect, and support. Far from being a sugar cookie, feedback is an honest, clear, adult-to-adult exchange about specific behaviour and the effects of those behaviour. The assumption is that both parties have positive intentions to do what is right for the company and other people.

Another assumption is that well-meaning people can have legitimate differences in perception. The person offering the feedback owns the feedback as it is his reaction to the behaviour of another person.

That is, the giver recognizes the fact that what is being offered is a perception and not an absolute fact."

Regular feedback will lead to a more open exchange of ideas and thoughts. Do keep the feedback precise and practical. Be sincere, genuine, humble and empathetic. Cliché, inanity or connote feedbacks are never obliging. Ensure that your feedback is clear without being overly simple or complex. Concentrate on how the performance of the student can be improved.

Seth Godin's Rules for Giving Great Feedback

- No one cares about your opinion. We want your analysis.
- Say the right thing at the right time.
- If you have something nice to say, please say it.
- Give feedback, no matter what.

## Canon 2: Encourage feedback from students

*"Champions know that success is inevitable; that there is no such thing as failure, only feedback. They know that the best way to forecast the future is to create it."*

*– Michael J. Gelb.*

Promote sincere and honest criticism from those students whose opinion you trust. Allow them to speak their mind, discuss their ideas, views, opinions and discuss suggestions.

Regularly organize brainstorming sessions for students. However, do not rely entirely on the outcomes of such sessions. As A. Harvey Block, American Business Executive, CEO of Bokenon Systems Inc feels, the ideas that come out of most brainstorming sessions are usually superficial, trivial, and not very original. The process, however, seems to make uncreative people feel that they are making innovative contributions and that others are listening to them. This will enable them to think creatively.

The same principle can be applied to any educational institution. Don't jump to any conclusion. Make students discuss what they think.

Along with this, frequently hold one-on-one meetings with every student to understand them.

Student's feedback can help teachers to understand their strengths and weaknesses so that they can enhance their teaching abilities. For example, you can regularly ask your students to fill out a questionnaire and give suggestions on how to improve their learning experience.

A good teacher, through appropriate feedback from students, identifies his/her strengths and limitations, analyzes and evaluates them and finds strengths an suitable solutions to overcome their weaknesses and build on their strengths. Research has revealed a direct positive correlation between students feeling connected to the institution and their internal motivation. This relationship can be developed by a teacher's kindness, honesty, sincerity, zeal, support and cooperative nature.

## Canon 3: Understand students' requirement

*"I have come to believe that a great teacher is a great artist and that they are as few as there are any other great artists. Teaching might even be the greatest of the arts. Since the medium is the human mind and spirit"*

*- John Steinbeck.*

To understand students' motivational factors, I conducted a survey to identify various aspects that influence students. According to my survey, the 5 most crucial elements were:-

a) Their personal interest in the subject/ topic.

b) Significance of the topic.

c) Self confidence of the teacher.

d) Knowledge of the teacher.

e) Endurance or fortitude of the teacher.

However, different students strive for different objectives in the classroom. Some of them are:-

i. To learn something new.

ii. To enhance their knowledge, skills and expertise.

iii. To overcome future hurdles.

iv. To become proficient.

v. To achieve growth in career.

To meet up with the above expectations, a teacher must be proactive and must upgrade his/her knowledge and skills regularly. Learn things that are really important and that would enhance your productivity. The more updated you are, the more certain you'll be. Whenever you learn something, think of different ways to apply your learning to benefit the students. Be ready to go that extra mile for your students.

Each day, add value to the work you are doing, since the best reward of a thing well done is to have it done. As rightly said by Robert H. Shaffer, we must view young people not as empty bottles to be filled, but as candles to be lit.

Personal targets and ambitions, past experiences, areas of interest, cultural background, age, academic ability levels, mental fitness, and behavioural problems vary the effect of classroom teaching and also determine a student's learning ability. Hence, it is essential for the teacher to identify student needs and make suitable modifications and adjustments in the teaching plan.

## Canon 4: Encourage active participation

*Research has shown that good everyday teaching practices can do more to counter student apathy than special efforts to attack motivation directly"*
*– Barbara Gross Davis in Erickson, 1978.*

Some students are unsurprisingly keen to learn, but most of them need someone who can constantly encourage, engage, excite, confront and kindle them. However there is no magic wand for building high self esteem and confidence in students. It's a gradual, step-by-step procedure which requires patience.

Many factors (some of which are stated earlier) like interest in the subject, perception of its future utility, desire to score good marks, keenness to enhance knowledge upgrade skills, self-confidence, self-esteem, fulfillment and enjoyment, plays key roles in invigorating students. Create a congenial and positive environment for students. Make teaching an enjoyable experience for the students. Be straightforward and always to the point.

Practice what you preach; set an example for students. Never lie and encourage students to speak the truth. Always fulfill your promises. Never make others feel inferior. An enthusiastic teacher with zest can easily convert a boring subject to an interesting one.

To inspire students to become independent, teachers can stimulate involvement in students. Ask them to always keep in mind the Chinese proverb, 'one who asks is a fool for five minutes, but he who does not ask remains a fool forever'. A teacher can contribute a lot to enhance a student's motivation. Persuade them to take their own decisions. Constantly ask questions and clear their doubts.

The level of motivation among each student in the class may differ drastically. However, it is the duty of a teacher to maintain the curiosity of the attentive students and convert the disinterested students into inquisitive ones. Participation generates curiosity among students. Continuously motivate them by saying, "you can do it". Ask your library to subscribe to some newsletters, journals, newspapers, magazines and encourage students to read them.

Hearten a two-way communication with the students as they learn faster from conversations. This can be done by,

- Occasionally asking their opinions.
- Cheering their ideas and views.
- Discussing important news and events with them.
- Encouraging feedback.
- Keeping them informed about the recent developments in your subject.

## Canon 5: Set reasonable expectations from students

There comes a time when you have to stand up and shout, 'This is me! I look the way I look, think the way I think, feel the way I feel, love the way I love! I am a whole complex package. Take me... or leave me. Accept me - or walk away! Do not try to make me feel like a lesser being, just because I don't fit your idea of who I should be. Don't try to change me to fit your mould. If I need to change, I alone will make that decision'.

In any class, there are varied types of students. Some students may understand slower than others. Don't stress them too much. Never be too much of a fault finder. Look for positives in every student. Set realistic goals for students based on their competency and ability. Decide in advance what you want to teach them the next day and make sure you achieve your target. Students are dependent on teachers, so teachers must be prepared always.

Allow students to be themselves. Unviable and impractical goals can dishearten and upset them. However, very low expectations from them can also lower their standards. Explain to them the famous quote of Ralph Marston, "Don't lower your expectations to meet your performance. Raise your level of performance to meet your expectations. Expect the best of yourself, and then do what is necessary to make it a reality".

If some students are good at math and others are not, you have to accept that. You have to accept that many students are not going to be as brilliant, gritty, striving, intelligent as others. So the level of expectations should vary. You have to respect their differences. Avoid generating extreme competition among students.

Delegate some task to the students to demonstrate your faith. Draft your weekly/ monthly plan in advance. Always have contingency plan, Keep a record of everything you do and say for future reference.

## Canon 6: Analyze the Strengths and Weaknesses of each student

*"If a man is called to be a street sweeper, he should sweep streets even as Michelangelo painted, or Beethoven composed music, or Shakespeare wrote poetry. He should sweep streets so well that all the hosts of heaven and earth will pause to say, here lived a great street sweeper who did his job well." - Martin Luther King.*

Try to understand the strengths and weaknesses of each student. Once you understand it, focus on their strengths to overcome their weaknesses. Don't compare them with others. Accept their weaknesses. With each lecture, gradually increase the difficulty level. Before preparing for each lecture, evaluate the needs, expectations, strengths, weaknesses, experience, expertise of the students in the class. St. Francis of Assisi once said, 'Start by doing what is necessary, then what is possible, and suddenly you are doing the impossible'.

At this point, I would like to make an interesting correlation between students and corporate managers. Berlin Meredith in his book, "Why they succeed or fail" has identified nine team roles for corporate managers. They can be categorized as:-

I. The resource investigator:- a creative individual.

II. The co-coordinator:- a highly disciplined and controlled individual.

III. The plant:- the original thinker.

IV. The team worker:- a highly supportive and cooperative person.

V. The specialist:- an extremely specialized and professional person.

VI. The sharper:- an individual who loves challenges

VII. The monitor evaluators:- an analytical thinker.

VIII. The implementer:- an individual who likes to get the work done.

IX. The completer:- a person who checks each and every minute detail.

On close observation, you will notice that this categorization applies to students as well. With the help of these nine team roles, a teacher can very easily identify the category for each student and work accordingly.

## Canon 7: Encourage self-enthusiasm among students

*"When you are strong enough to love yourself 100%, good and bad – you will be amazed at the opportunities that life presents you."*
*– Stancey Charter.*

Young students are usually full of inquisitiveness. But regrettably, as they grow, their excitement for education minimizes. Repeatedly, they associate studying with pressure rather than pleasure. If observed carefully, most of them are just physically present and mentally absent in the class. Hence, it is very important to involve them in studies.

Remind them the words of George Gritter that a duty which becomes a desire will ultimately become a delight.

Share some jokes and enjoy yourself. Have a sense of humor. Be sincere and not serious. Maintain a good relationship with the students. If you make a mistake, accept it and try to rectify it.

Even though students may be equally motivated to perform or to study, the level of their motivation may be different. Students who are internally motivated will study for knowledge, self development, enjoyment, enhancement of skills, or even for the feeling of achievement but an "externally" motivated student performs for better marks, grades and even to avoid punishment. A school should foster self esteem, proficiency, independence, self-efficiency, self confidence and self respect among its students.

Let me here reiterate the famous poem of Dorothy Law Nolte:-

Children Learn What They Live

If children live with criticism, they learn to condemn.
If children live with hostility, they learn to fight.
If children live with fear, they learn to be apprehensive.
If children live with pity, they learn to feel sorry for themselves.
If children live with ridicule, they learn to feel shy.
If children live with jealousy, they learn to feel envy.
If children live with shame, they learn to feel guilty.
If children live with encouragement, they learn confidence.
If children live with tolerance, they learn patience.

If children live with praise, they learn appreciation.

If children live with acceptance, they learn to love.

If children live with approval, they learn to like themselves.

If children live with recognition, they learn it is good to have a goal.

If children live with sharing, they learn generosity.

If children live with honesty, they learn truthfulness.

If children live with fairness, they learn justice.

If children live with kindness and consideration, they learn respect.

If children live with security, they learn to have faith
in themselves and in those about them.

If children live with friendliness, they learn the world
is a nice place in which to live.

## Canon 8: Avoid giving answers first

*"I consider my ability to arouse enthusiasm among men the greatest asset I possess. The way to develop the best that is in a man is by appreciation and encouragement."*

*– Charles Schwab.*

Avoid giving answers first. If you directly give solutions to any question, students will never make an attempt to find the solution. Tell the students to make an attempt first. Tolerance is vital. Persuade them to come up with a solution and then you try to solve them. Allow them to speculate the outcome of any discussion/debate. Always remember, without the right questions, you'll never be able to get the right answers.

Don't use marks as "fear motivation" for students. Accept responsibility for your student's poor performance. Just because they failed, it doesn't mean that they didn't work hard. As said by Wooden Wilson, 'I would rather fail in a cause that will ultimately succeed than succeed in a cause that would ultimately fail'.

Teach them that life is a great journey. Problem is that it doesn't come with a map and instructions, we have to make our own way and God will help only those who help themselves. Encourage them to find the solutions to any question. Listen to them if you want them to listen to you. Delegate some task to them to demonstrate your faith in them.

## Canon 9: Teach them the importance of positive attitude

*"A man lost almost everything in a fire. Next day he placed a signboard Shop burnt! House burnt! Goods burnt! But faith not burnt..Shop starts tomorrow."*

A great thinker was asked, "What is the meaning of life?" he replied – "Life itself has no meaning. Life is an opportunity to create meaning."

Let me share with you a small anecdote of legendary Wimbledon player Arthur Ashe who died of an HIV infection. He received millions of letters from his fans. One of them said: "Do you ever ask God, 'why me?'." He replied, "50 million children watch tennis, 5 million learn to play tennis, 50,000 learn professional tennis, 5000 come to the circuit, 500 reach the grand slam, 50 reach the Wimbledon, only 4 reach the semi-finals and 2 reach the finals and when I was holding that cup, I never asked God, "Why me? So why should I now?"

Ensure that they don't bank too much on luck. Nothing is impossible as the word itself says that I'm possible. So tell them never to completely surrender themselves to fate or destiny. Lucille Ball once quoted: "Luck? I don't know anything about luck. I've never banked on it and I'm afraid of people who do. Luck to me is something else: Hard work - and realizing what opportunity is and what isn't".

Spread a smile, its contagious. Be passionate and excited; occasionally change your teaching technique as well. Never abuse other teachers or colleagues.

Our actions are constantly affected by our negative beliefs, past mistakes and future apprehension. But, this problem can be easily solved by cultivating positive thoughts and focusing on individual goals. If they don't believe in themselves then how can they expect others to believe in them.

The following techniques help build a positive attitude.

- Inculcating a habit of doing their work without procrastination.
- Training them to stay away from negative influences.
- Motivating them to read biographies of successful people.
- Teaching them that they shouldn't waste what they have, by desiring for what they don't have.
- Instructing them that whenever they are disheartened, they should keep their long term goal in mind and move on.

## Canon 10: Be their genuine friend, philosopher and guide

*"To a very large degree, students expect to learn if the teachers expect them to learn"*
*– Deboran Stipek.*

Being a teacher is not child's play. A teacher is expected to be an organizer, a trendsetter, a representative, a guardian and a specialist.

They are responsible for the physical, mental and emotional development of entire class. A teacher is the connecting link between educational institutions and students.

A teacher plays a very significant role in the life of a student. According to Jere Brophy (1987), motivation to learn is a competence acquired "through general experience but stimulated most directly through modeling, communication of expectations and direct instruction or socialization by significant others (parents and teachers.)". A teacher's knowledge, attitude, perception, behaviour, technique and style of interaction can easily transform the level of a student's motivation for better by making them understand how their learning can be applied in real world.

Discuss but never argue with them. Control your temper If students in your class openly disagree with your statement, don't shout at them or impose your ideas. On the other hand, appreciate them and then explain your point of view.

A teacher should inspire, lead, motivate, and challenge the students to get emotionally involved in any task they pursue. Share your knowledge as much as you can. Set your own standards and never try to intimate others. Be aware of your duties and responsibilities.

It's not what you say; it's the things
you do, that makes someone feel
confident in you. Nice words all of
us like to hear. But actions speak
louder than words I fear. Words,
how easy they are to say. For
some, it's all they can show. As
for me, I prefer the silent type,
by their actions, they're sure to
let you know. Those of you, who
feel listening to nice words is
quite important. At some point,
I'd have to agree. However, to
be able to show how you feel
by your actions, well now....
that speaks louder to me!

-Audrey Heller

## Canon 11: Empower them to help themselves

*You see things; and you say, "Why"?*
*But I dream things that never were; and I say "Why not"?*
*– George Bernard Shaw.*

Support them to help themselves and their friends to constantly enhance, upgrade and update their knowledge and not only grades. Facilitate them to achieve their goals. Ensure that they are always ready to learn, unlearn and relearn. Identify when they are stressed and allow them to take a break. Encourage them to follow their intuitions and gut feeling.

As rightly said by someone, 'be thankful to God that you don't have everything you want. It means you still have an opportunity to be happier tomorrow than you are today. Today, common sense is the most uncommon thing. A desire can change nothing, but a decision can change something. Make them share their knowledge, ability, idea and skill. Every small contribution they make can make a big difference in others life.

Prepare them to be reliable in any uncertain and unpredictable situation. Train them to always give their best. Prepare them for the ups and downs in life as life is full of pains and pleasures. Make them proactive and not reactive.

Life runs on two simple rules - "accept" and "change". "Accept" the things which you can't "change" or "change" the things you can't "accept."

## Canon 12: Make them believe in themselves

*"Do all the good you can. By all the means you can. In all the ways you can. In all the places you can. At all the times you can. To all the people you can. As long as ever you can."*

*— John Wesley.*

Teach them to exult even during tough times, as the one who can be happy even during crisis, ultimately succeeds in life. Inculcate "self-confidence" among students. Tell them that the beginning of all tasks is small, but beginning is never a small task; so enjoy simple pleasures of life. Make them emotionally, physically and morally involved in any task. As rightly said by Benedict Spinoza, "... to become what we are capable of becoming is the only end to life."

Teach them to be passionate and follow their dreams. Success is the vehicle which moves on a wheel named "smart work" – but the journey is impossible without the fuel named "self confidence." Birds find shelter during rain, but the eagle avoids rain by flying above the clouds.

Instruct them to keep a check on their weight and take care of their health. Tutor them to say "no" whenever they disagree with something or somebody. Teach them to take a calculated risk.

**ONLY A PERSON WHO RISKS IS FREE**

**by Joan Gadsby**

To laugh is to risk appearing the fool.
To weep is to risk appearing sentimental.
To reach for another is to risk involvement.
To expose your ideas, your dreams,
before a crowd is to risk their loss.
To love is to risk not being loved in return.
To live is to risk dying.
To believe is to risk despair.

To try is to risk failure.
But risks must be taken, because the
greatest hazard in life is to risk nothing.
The people, who risk nothing, do nothing,
have nothing, are nothing.
They may avoid suffering and sorrow,
but they cannot learn, feel, change,
grow, love, live.
Chained by their attitudes they are slaves;
they have forfeited their freedom
Only a person who risks is free.

Understand what they love to do. Encourage creativity to make each day exciting. Encourage innovative thoughts and ideas. Appreciate innovation. Put their names or photogtaphs along with their work on the notice board or the institution's newsletter. Create an environment where ideas are recognized.

Train them to be flexible, to adopt new changes and accept them as a part of their lives. Twisted but beautiful lines, "Changing the face can change nothing but facing the change can change everything."

## Canon 13: Let them plan each day in advance

*"He slept beneath the moon, he basked beneath the sun;*
*he lived a life of going to do and died with nothing done"*
*– James Albery.*

Teach them to prioritize their task. Tell them not to worry too much about future and give their best each day. Use their energy for constructive work today rather than anticipating too much about their future. Edify them to focus on things that are really important.

Help them to plan their short term and long term career goals. Their career plans designed today will decide their fortune tomorrow, but tell them that there is 'no substitute' for hard work. As said by Les Brown, "your goals are the road maps that guides you and shows you what is possible for your life." Their goals are the targets they are striving to achieve, without which they are aimless. The best example is of sports. There can be no game without concrete goals or targets. Similarly every individual needs some targets.

You have to instruct them that just setting a goal is not enough. They must have a detailed blue print/ game plan to achieve their goal. They should break their targets into smaller goals. Tell them that the best source of motivation is working for a pre-determined objective. Such goals give an individual a strong point to face a tricky and complex situation in life.

Time is precious, so teach them to use it to effeciently. To make realize of the value of time, remind them the following.

To realize the value of ONE YEAR
– Ask a student who has failed his final exam.

To realize the value of ONE MONTH
– Ask a mother who has given birth to a premature baby.

To realize the value of ONE WEEK
– Ask an editor of a weekly newspaper.

To realize the value of ONE DAY
– Ask a daily wage labourer who has ten kids to feed.

To realize the value of ONE HOUR
– Ask the lovers who are waiting to meet.

To realize the value of ONE MINUTE
– Ask a person who has missed the train.

To realize the value of ONE SECOND
– Ask a person who has survived an accident.

To realize the value of ONE MILLISECOND
– Ask the person who has won a silver medal in the Olympics.

*Treasure every moment that you have! And treasure it more because you share it with someone special ... special enough to have your time. . ....Anonymous*

Make them understand that "all work and no play" makes Jack a dull boy and factors like health, physical exercise, mental state, diet (eating habits) and surroundings do have an impact on their lives. Train them to be versatile by exploring their colossal talent.

Educate them to inculcate any new hobbies like painting, reading, singing, sports etc. Prepare them to maintain a balance between academics and extra-curricular activities because a healthy mind lives in a healthy body. Instruct them to use their time effectively and efficiently.

On a lighter note, share with them the following equation: Students law of tension:- Pressure is inversely proportional to the number of days left for the exams, where "I will definitely start my studies from tomorrow" remains constant.

## Canon 14: Make them face fear to overcome it

*Everyone has inside of him a piece of good news. The good news is that you don't know how great you can be! How much you can love! What you can accomplish! And what your potential is!"*

*– Anne Frank*

Develop an "I will", "I can", "I should", "I have" approach in students. Make them believe in themselves. Let them take their own decisions, which may be wrong sometimes. Tell them that it takes a lot of courage and self belief to do things that we really believe in. As rightly said by Michelangelo, "the greatest danger for most of us is not that our aim is too high and we miss it, but that it is too low and we reach it".

Tutor them that they shouldn't be disappointed if the world refuses to help them. Instead, they should remember the words of Albert Einstein, "I'm thankful to all those who said No. It's because of them I did it myself". Allow them to make mistakes. Let them learn from their mistakes and make sure that they never repeat them again. Inculcate in them the power of persistence.

Tell them that it doesn't matter how many times they fall, what counts is how many times they bounce back after they fall. Ensure that they learn to apologise for their mistakes as well. Let them set their own standards. Make certain that they constantly try to raise their standards, but see to it that they are not disheartened by failures. Make them count their blessings and not their problems. Teach them to accept others limitations and drawbacks, as life is best for those who enjoy it, difficult for those who analyze it, worst for those who criticize it.

**Teacher Says, Teacher Goes**

Teacher says,
teacher goes,
teacher smiles,
teacher knows,
what you have done,
was clearly a mistake,
maybe it is,
time for a break.

Teacher says,
teacher goes,
teacher smiles,
teacher knows,

that you have been naughty.
That you have been quite foughty.
That you are being rude,
don't call teacher a dude.

Teacher says,
teacher goes,
teacher smilies,
teacher know,

that you were making faces,
behind teacher's back,
that you were throwing spitballs,
at the teacher's pet.

Teacher says,
teacher goes,
teacher smiles,
teacher knows.
So enough is said,
so now you know,
that whatever you do.....

Teacher says,
Teacher goes,
Teacher smilies,
Teacher knows

- Jasmine Aira

## Canon 15: Build their character

*"Watch your thoughts, for they become words.*
*Watch your words, for they become actions.*
*Watch your actions, for they become habits.*
*Watch your habits, for they become character.*
*Watch your character, for it becomes your destiny."*

*– Frank Outlaw.*

Inspire loyalty and honesty. Teach them to respect values and principles. Inculcate high ethical and moral values among students. Encourage them to live a life of pride and honor. In the words of Thomas Jefferson, "In matters of style, swim with the current; in matter of principle, stand like a rock star." Simplicity is a vital ingredient for success. Character is more important than reputation, because character is what we really are, while reputation is only what others think we are.

Make them aware of their responsibilities. Touching only the sky doesn't define success; success will be when we don't take our feet off the ground, while touching the sky. Team them to work in harmony.

Develop team spirit among students. Create an atmosphere where everyone encourages each other and celebrate their success together.

If they dislike someone, tell them to identify the reason for the same:-

- Does the other lack enthusiasm?
- Is he/she unsure?
- Does he/she lack man management?
- Does he/she never accept responsibility?
- Does he/she always demotivates others?
- Does he/she never discuss new ideas?

After identifying the reason, ask them to find some strategy to overcome the problem. Sucsess comes through conscious efforts of planning + evaluating + interpretating and taking correct decisions. Efforts and rewards are two sides of the same coin. Failures are never stumbling blocks to success. So never lose hope or get demoralized by failures. Determination is very vital for success, since no flowery path leads to success. Teach students that success is the combination of positive attitude, self confidence, hard work and understanding. Success has three basic components, goals, willingness and strategy. The more willingness you have, the lesser obstacles you see. It helps to overcome past failures as well.

# 9 Ways to be a Good Colleague

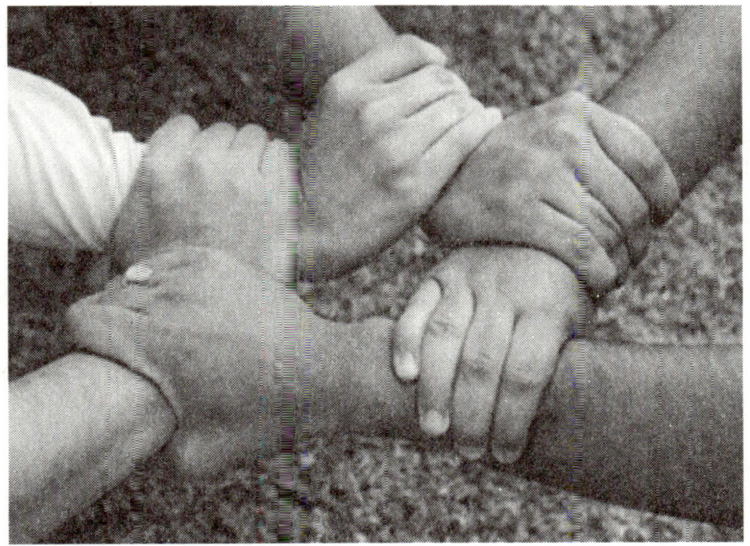

## Rule 1: Practice good workplace etiquettes

Good etiquettes are very important. The word "etiquette" is derived from French which actually means a "ticket", your ticket to getting anything and anyplace you want. It refers to norms and standards of behaviour that is socially acceptable.

Research conducted by Harvard University shows that technical skills and knowledge account for only 15% of getting, keeping and advancing in a job. 85% of the job success is connected to soft skills. This research significantly highlights the importance of etiquette that includes courtesy, image, trust and reliability. It increases opportunities for new ideas, fosters congenial work place relationship, builds confidence and creates goodwill.

India is one of the largest countries and business culture here tends to be more informal and friendly.

Certain personality traits of Indian nationals:

- There are more than 14 major and 300 minor languages spoken in India. The official languages are English and Hindi. English is widely used in business and education.
- Many Indians are vegetarians.
- Favourite topics of conversation are Politics, Family, Cricket, Bollywood and Films.
- Whistling is considered as Impolite.
- Alcohol is usually avoided at lunch; Indian women are not always comfortable drinking in public.
- Breakfast and Dinner meetings are rare and usually business lunch is preferred.
- Business decisions are mostly made at higher level.
- The country's most important festival is Diwali, when business associate exchange small gifts, sweets or dry fruits. It is considered auspicious especially to start a new venture.

Etiquettes are dependent on culture, what is excellent etiquette in one society may be rude in other. Hence, understanding the culture of India is a key to successful business relationship. There are certain etiquettes which may vary by region, institute size, institute policy, rules and regulations. However, general business etiquettes in India are:-

- Gifts are not opened in the presence of the giver.
- Acceptable gifts are flowers, chocolates and perfumes.
- "I will try" is an acceptable refusal rather than "No".
- Putting hands on hips is rude.
- Confidential matters should be kept in few hands as it can be used against the interest of the institute.

In the modern world, if the institute is able to deal with e-mails effectively, then they can gain a competitive edge and achieve professionalism. While replying to an e-mail, click "reply" instead of "new mail". Make your subject line specific, meaningful and don't type in all CAPS as it seems loud. Avoid errors such as spelling errors, improper grammar and punctuation as it can sometimes change the meaning of the text. Customize your mail and be concise. The following are some e-mail etiquettes.

Don't attach unnecessary files/ documents with your e-mail. Take care with abbreviations and emoticons. Use proper structure and layout. Use active instead of passive voice, avoid long sentences and repetitive use of words like urgent and important.

Never write e-mails to discuss confidential information; answer swiftly; don't reply to spam and never copy attachments or messages without permission.

For effective meetings, communicate beforehand the objective, expected duration and the issues expected to be discussed. Make it a point to arrive 10-15 minutes before a meeting and introduce yourself to the other participants. A short and light and not firm handshake is the customary start to the meeting and a non-verbal clue of a friendly deal.

Make sure to thank the members for their time and participation. Show them how their contribution helped in achieving the objectives of the meeting. Avoid arranging your meetings on national holidays and don't bring your cell phones to meetings. Avoid wearing too much perfume or chewing gum during meetings or lectures.

There are certain telephone etiquettes which one needs to follow. Communication over phone requires the use of non-verbal skills such as a pleasant tone, impressive voice, proper intonation and clear articulation of words.

Before initiating a call, prepare yourself about what is your purpose of call. A confident self-introduction always makes a positive impression. Introduce yourself in a slow, clear manner and don't use words such as Mr., Ms, Mrs., Shri, Smt or even Prof. while referring to yourself, you can call other people by such titles.

The most important things to remember is to be considerate, courteous, diplomatic and thoughtful to the people around you, regardless of the circumstances. Address the conflicts as situation-related rather than people-related and never differentiate the people by their position within the institute. Treat all colleagues with respect and regard.

Always speak well, don't leak and pass along credit to everyone who has made a contribution. Remember not to take credit for your co-workers contribution to a project.

Avoid chewing gum and asking questions to colleagues about their family size, marital status and religion. Never tell dirty jokes or forward dirty e-mails. Don't talk about your institute, other colleagues or seniors behind their backs – as not being involved in such activities minimizes irritation among your colleagues and contributes to a positive work environment.

For any college party, carry your business card and never use foul language or tell dirty jokes. Don't wear suggestive or revealing clothes, and never gossip. The basic knowledge and practice of etiquette is a valuable advantage, because in a lot of situations, a second chance is not given.

Finally, every institute has certain written and unwritten rules which apply to every single aspect of work viz. how to e-mail, talk on phone, conduct oneself in a meeting, business party and group conversations.

## Rule 2: Practice good telephone etiquettes

As rightly said, "Manners maketh a man". The English dictionary describes "Etiquettes" as the rules for socially acceptable behaviour. It refers to certain norms, standards and code of conduct that guides an individual and shows him/her how to behave with others. The various types of etiquettes are dining etiquettes, telephone etiquettes, meeting etiquettes, party etiquettes, e-mail etiquettes, so on and so forth.

Here are a few telephone etiquettes which one must remember.

1. Avoid using cell phones at hospitals, interviews, funerals, temples, flights, cinema theatres, concert halls, while driving, during meetings, seminars and lectures.
2. Before making any call; know the receiver and the purpose of the call.
3. Prepare and draft the structure of the conversation before the call as the call should be short, sensible and to the point.
4. Learn to say "thank-you", "sorry" and "you are welcome".
5. Be patient, cheerful, polite, friendly and enthusiastic.
6. Speak clearly with confidence to avoid misunderstanding or misinterpretation and use appropriate non-verbal communication like proper tone/pitch and modulation of voice.
7. Never use slang, don't shout or scream on the phone.
8. Repeat the key points, if necessary.
9. Know the right time to call the concerned person.
10. Don't be rude to the caller; be considerate, calm and courteous.
11. If you don't know the caller; ask his/her name, name of his/her institute, his/her designation and the purpose of calling.
12. Finally, be an active and attentive listener, don't interrupt the conversation.

## Rule 3: Learn good communication skills

> *"Your ability to communicate is an important tool in the pursuit of your goals, whether it is with your family, your co-workers or your clients and customers."*
>
> *– Les Brown.*

For any teacher, good communication skills (whether oral or written) is a must. According to Robert Anderson, "Communication is an interchange of thoughts, opinions, or information, through speech, writing or signs". Written Communication means communication by means of written symbols (either printed or handwritten).

Here are certain golden rules of effective written communication:-

- There are several types of written communication in business like e-mail message, memos, proposals, reports, letters, bulletins, minutes, orders, quotations, contracts, forms, enquiries etc. Poorly written messages create confusion and misunderstanding. Hence, understanding the purpose, the audience, the message and the channel is essential.
- M.K Sehgal and Vandana Khetarpal have mentioned several advantages and disadvantages of written communication which are briefed below:

**Advantages:-**

1. Ready reference.
2. Legal defense.
3. Promotes uniformity.
4. Mass access.
5. Suitable for distance communication.
6. Image building.
7. Accurate and unambiguous.
8. Permanent in nature.
9. Facilitates to assign responsibility.
10. Permits substitutions and revisions.

**Disadvantages:-**

1. Limited to literate world.
2. Time Consuming.
3. Lot of paper work.
4. Needs expertise in expression.
5. Lacks immediate feedback
6. Costlier than oral communication.
7. More man hours needed.
8. No immediate clarification.

**TIPS for effective Written Communication:-**

- Draft an outline at the beginning by proper planning.
- Focus on the audience, purpose, topic and desired outcome. "Simply writing or talking, without regard to the recipients' response, is conducive to creating a gross misunderstanding" – George Terry.
- Structure the introduction, body and conclusion in a systematic and logical order.
- Focus on each paragraph.
- Understand the reader's perception.
- Avoid grammatical errors.
- Use proper vocabulary and punctuations.
- Avoid using slang.
- Avoid using "you" in criticism.
- Always start on a positive note.
- Always write the name of the company and the person correctly.

- Keep sentences short, clear and concise.
- Avoid repetition and too many irrelevant details.
- Elaborate on the technical language and jargons used.
- Effectively use the charts, graphs, diagrams and pictures.
- Never express your anger, frustration, irritation and aggression in written communication.
- Proof read the document before sending.
- Use proper communication channel.
- Get a proper feedback.
- Continuously update yourself to improve your written skills.

I would conclude by the famous words of Alexander Pope, "True ease in writing comes from art, not chance, as those move easiest, who have learnt to dance".

## Learn the art of writing formal letters

*"Doing something efficiently is doing it right, but doing it effectively is doing it well"*
*- Anonymous*

An effective letter is a carrier of goodwill. Letters are the most important form of business correspondence since the organization has to keep in touch with the world outside like the university, press, other institutes, parents etc.

It can be further classified on the basis of their subject, viz. enquiries, information, collection of dues, complaints, promotion, circulars, appointment of personnel and so on. They can also be classified on the basis of the correspondence of different departments of an institute.

The language, content, style, length, structure, layout, tone and purpose of a letter are essential to create a good impact. Clarify your purpose of writing - whether it is to inform, invite, reiterate, emphasize, remind, announce or to seek permission. Keep in mind the reader and put yourself in the reader's shoes while writing. Analyze the skills, knowledge, status and ability of the addressee. "A good letter shows consideration and thoughtfulness, it uses "you" more frequently than "I". Check the phrases, words, grammar and spelling since mistakes, corrections, striking and overwriting create a poor impact. Have a powerful vocabulary".

Simplicity, elegance, decency and brevity are hallmarks of a good letter. As said by William Shakespeare, brevity is the soul of wit. A communication is said to be concrete when it is specific, sharp, focused, definite and to the point. Always emphasize on the positive. Stress on what you can do for the reader and not what you cannot do. Always stay away from negative words and phrases.

Before you begin writing, decide your purpose and the reader's needs by answering all the following W's and H (why, when, where, who, what and how). Decide what you want to write in first paragraph, the main body (heart of the letter), and conclusion. These may vary, from the conversational style often found in e-mail messages, to the more formal style found in legal documents.

Letter head (heading), reference number, date, inside address of the institute, name and address of the receiver, attention line, subject line, salutation, complimentary close, signature with date and designation, reference section (enclosure, courtesy copy) are all the parts of an effective letter. For an accurate E-mail, format the information, keep the contents brief, don't use capitals and don't get too informal.

Notification of attachments or additional information is included at the very end of the letter. Finally, evaluate whether you have included all the relevant information and has it accomplished your purpose.

**Do's of an Effective Letter:-**

- Be straight forward, focused, specific and never manipulate.
- Use short and simple words with correct meaning, punctuations and relevance.
- Use short, crisp and succinct paragraphs.
- Effectively use pronouns and active voice; minimize use of passive voice.
- The tone should be, cordial, polite, courteous and kind.
- Practice consistency, accuracy and perseverance in writing.
- Try to keep your letter to one page. If the letter continues on the second page, don't use letterhead.
- Follow the 7 C's of Business writing:- clear, concise, correct, courteous, conventional, convincing and complete.
- Emphasize on good quality of paper, letter head, layout, colour, size, spacing, design and margins.
- Proofread it carefully.

**Dont's of an effective letter:-**

- Use bombastic Language.
- Begin every paragraph with the word "I".
- Write unnecessary information and repetition of words.
- Use emoticons and acronyms.

Here are certain tips for making an effective oral presentation.

- An oral presentation is explained as a talk given to a group in which an individual presents his/her view on an issue or a topic based on his/her reading or research.
- Teachers needs good communication skills to interact with their superiors / subordinates and even students, to convey their information effectively in the institute's meetings / presentations / seminars, for proper planning, organization, co-ordination, leadership, motivation and controlling.

Here are few tips which a teacher needs to follow for a powerful oral communication.

## 1. Before the Presentation

- Know your objective, audience, the total time allotted for the message to be conveyed and the resources available. Systematically and logically frame the three main parts of the presentation viz. the introduction, the main body and the conclusion.
- Rehearse and practice the entire presentation.
- Anticipate few questions and prepare their answers.
- Prepare a contingency plan.

## 2. During the Presentation

- Check the equipments, room arrangement and the lay-out.
- Use proper visual aids, diagrams, pictures, graphs, facts, figures, over head projector and power point presentation (templates, design and font).
- Take some deep breath before starting.
- Stay confident, relaxed and be enthusiastic.
- Keep it simple, be concise, to the point and avoid repetition.
- Explain the key points with appropriate stories, examples, anecdotes and demonstrations.
- Emphasize on the key points.
- Never read continuously from the script.
- Use appropriate humour.
- Avoid using too many technical details.
- Emphasize on proper body movement, tone, eye contact, posture and gestures.
- Conclude on time.
- Leave time for discussion and for clarification of doubts.

## 3. After the Presentation

- Allow question and answer sessions.
- If you don't know the answer, don't lie.
- Take proper audience feedback.
- Find out areas of improvement.

A research has found that the important elements of communication identified by small, medium and large institutes.They are as follows.

- Listening and understanding
- Speaking clearly and directly

- Writing to the needs of the audience
- Negotiating responsively
- Reading independently
- Empathizing
- Using numeracy effectively
- Understanding the needs of internal and external customers
- Persuading effectively
- Establishing and using networks
- Being assertive
- Sharing information and
- Speaking and writing in languages other than English.

Similarly, learn the art of public speaking

As rightly said, "Half the world is composed of people who have something to say and can't; the other half have nothing to say and keep saying it." Public Speaking is explained as the process of speaking to a group of people in a structured, deliberate manner intended to inform, influence, or entertain the listener. It is a powerful tool used for various purposes such as motivation, influencing, persuasion, information, translation, entertainment etc.

A research revealed that 75% of the people suffer from "glossophopia" or "stage fright" which means fear of public speaking. Even the world's best speakers faced nervousness and stage fright. According to Mark Twain there are two types of speakers: those that are nervous and those that are liars. However, the good news is that you can overcome the fear through sincere efforts and by adopting the techniques stated below.

1. Understand the occasion, venue and the message to be conveyed before the speech.
2. Who are the listeners? What do you want to communicate? When do you want to convey the message? Where is the venue? Why should the audience listen to you? How will you convey the message? Ask yourself these questions.
3. Prepare yourself before the speech as the one who fails to prepare, prepares to fail.
4. Emphasize on your strengths to overcome the weaknesses.
5. Structure the opening, body and closing of the speech effectively.

6. Use proper body language, gestures, tones, facial expressions and eye contact with the audiences.
7. Speak clearly, i.e. neither too fast nor too slow.
8. Keep the sentences short and simple and don't read word-to-word from your notes or reference material.
9. Use appropriate graphs, diagrams, pictures, charts and other visual aids but don't over use them.
10. Support your statements with proper examples.
11. Don't get into arguments with the listener, if he/she disagrees with your ideas.
12. Stay relaxed, calm, be enthusiastic, positive and confident.
13. Know when to stop and keep a watch on time.
14. Allow a question and answer session in the end.
15. Always use language that you are comfortable with.
16. Finally, believe in what you are saying.

However, acknowledge the fact that non-verbal communication is equally important. No matter how much one can try, one cannot not-communicate. As described earlier, communication can be classified as verbal and non-verbal. Verbal communication is through words and speech, whereas non-verbal communication does not involve speech or words. It is a wordless message received through gestures, signs, body language, facial expressions, time, space, style of writing, clothing and personality.

Researches in communication suggest that more feelings and intentions are sent and received non-verbally than verbally. Mehrabian and Wiener suggested that only 7% of a message is sent through words while the remaining 93% is sent through non-verbal expressions; 55% through facial expression, body language, gestures and 38% through tone, accent and intonation.

Thus, the research suggests that non-verbal communication is more instinctive, powerful and genuine. Education psychologist Marilyn Maple says, "when you can consciously 'read', what others are saying unconsciously, you can deal with issues at work and at home before they turn into full blown problems".

Non-verbal communication can be classified as kinesics (use of body language which includes facial expression, eye contact, gestures, appearances), proxemics (use of space language, surrounding and environment); (effective time management); sign language (use of audio visuals) and haptics (use of "touch" language)

Many times, teachers tend to convey their feelings by smiling, patting, shouting, frowning or even by using different tones, gestures and facial expression to give a deeper meaning to their sentences. They communicate by the way they walk, stand and sit. Positive postures and movements are frequent indicators of self-confidence, energy, status, attitude, approval and warmth. Dressing identifies sex, age, socio-economic class, religion, status, role, group membership, occasion, personality, mood and physical environment.

Accent, intonation, pitch, speed of delivery and clarity are factors attributing to non-verbal communication. It is not what we say that counts, but how we say it". This reflects the significance of vocal intonation. Some words or phrases can have different meanings depending on how they are said. Difference in loudness, pitch, temper, rate, inflection, rhythm and enunciation all relate to the expression of various emotions.

'A picture is worth a thousand words' is a saying that conveys well the significance of facial expressions. Facial expressions may be intentional or unintentional. However, the most dominant and reliable features of the face are the eyes and the smile. The eyes provides a constant channel of communication. They can be shifty and evasive. They convey hate, fear and guilt, or express confidence, love and support. Smiling is a powerful positive cue that transmits happiness, friendliness, warmth, liking, affiliation and affection.

The importance of non-verbal communication is rightly explained by Nancy Austin, a management consultant. "When people don't know whether to believe what they are hearing or what they are seeing, they try to follow the non-verbal language which often tells the truth. You can play fast and get loose with words, but it's much more difficult to lose with gestures." observes Nancy.

Here are few tips for effective non-verbal communication.

1. Make yourself comfortable, relaxed and attentive.
2. Maintain frequent eye contact. Avoid staring, glaring or looking away.
3. Control the tone of your voice.
4. Gestures should not reveal emotional frustration.
5. Maintain a clear and audible voice.
6. Maintain a pleasant but genuine smile.

There can be certain barriers to effective communication as well, which a good teacher needs to identify and eliminate in order to communicate effectively.

D.E. McFarland has defined communication as the process of meaningful interaction among human beings. More specifically, it is the process by which meanings are perceived and understandings are reached among human beings. However there are some barriers in the communication system that prevent the message from reaching the receiver. These barriers are as follows.

## 1. Language Barriers

Different languages, vocabulary, accents and dialects pose national or regional barriers. Semantic gaps are words having similar pronunciation but multiple meanings. They result in badly expressed message, wrong interpretation and unqualified assumptions. The use of difficult or inappropriate words and poorly explained or misunderstood messages can result in confusion.

## 2. Cultural Barriers

Age, education, gender, socio-economic status, cultural background, temperament, health, beauty, popularity, religion, political belief, ethics, values, motives, assumptions, aspirations, rules, standards, priorities etc. can separate one person from another and create a barrier.

## 3. Individual Barriers

It may be a result of an individual's perceptual discomfort. Even when two people experience the same event, their mental perception may not be identical. This may act as a barrier. Style, selective perception, halo effect, poor attention and retention, defensiveness, close mindedness, insufficient filtration are all the individual or psychological barriers.

## 4. Institutional Barriers

It includes poor institution culture, climate, stringent rules, status, relationship, complexity, inadequate opportunities for growth and improvement. The nature of the internal and external environment of the institute in terms of large working areas that are physically separated from others, poor lighting, staff shortage, outdated equipments and background noise are physical institutional barriers.

## 5. Interpersonal Barriers

Barriers from employers include lack of trust in employees, lack of knowledge of non-verbal clues include different experiences, shortage of time for employees, no consideration for employee needs, wish to capture authority, fear of losing power of control, bypassing and information overloading. On the other hand, barriers from employees include lack of motivation, lack of co-operation, trust, fear of penalty and poor relationship with the employer.

## 6. Attitudinal Barriers

It comes about as a result of problems with staff in the institution. Limitation in physical and mental ability, intelligence, understanding, pre-conceived notions, and distrusted sources who divide the attention and create a mechanical barrier affecting one's attitude and opinions.

## 7. Channel Barriers

If the length of the communication is long, or the medium selected is inappropriate, the communication might break up. It can also be a result of the inter-personal conflicts between the sender and receiver, lack of interest to communicate, information sharing or access problems which can hamper the channel and affect its clarity, accuracy and effectiveness.

To communicate effectively, one needs to overcome these barriers. Working on breaking these barriers is a broad-brush activity and here are certain measures that can be taken to do so.

## Do's:

- Allow colleagues access to resources, self-expression and idea generation.
- Express your expectations to others.
- Use less of absolute words such as "never", "always", "forever", etc.
- Be a good, attentive and active listener.
- Filter the information correctly before passing it on to someone else.
- Try to establish one communication channel and eliminate the intermediaries.
- Use specific and accurate words which audiences can easily understand.
- Try and view the situations through the eyes of the speaker.
- The "you" attitude must be used on all occasions.
- Maintain eye contact with the speaker and make him comfortable.
- Write the instructions if the information is very detailed or complicated.
- Oral communication must be clear and not heavily accented.
- Avoid miscommunication of words and semantic noise.
- Ask for clarifications, repetition where necessary.
- Make the institutional structure more flexible, dynamic and transparent.
- Foster a congenial relationship which strengthens the coordination between superiors and subordinates.
- Focus on purposeful and focused communication.
- The message of communication should be clear and practical.
- Get proper feedback.

## Dont's:

- Be a selective listener. This is when a person hears another but selects not to listen what is being said, either by choice or desire to listen to some other message.
- Be a "Fixer". A fixer is a person that tries to find other person's fault.
- Be a daydreamer.
- Use long chain of commands for communication.
- Use too many technical jargons.
- Jump to conclusions immediately.
- Interrupt the speaker and distract him/her by asking too many irrelevant questions.

## Rule 4: Developing negotiation skills

According to Oxford dictionary, 'to negotiate' means to confer with another person with a view to compromise or to arrange or bring about agreement. Thus, negotiation means taking decision with an objective to create a "win-win" situation for both the parties; for mutual benefit and positive outcome. It also helps and save time and energy, reduce stress, encourage team spirit, enhances productivity and increase profitability.

In an educational institute, negotiations occur between teachers and management, students and management, teachers and students, administrative staff and management and other departments for appropriate allocation of resources. As said by Subhash Jagota, it is never easy to ask, but it is more difficult to give. Hence, master the art of give and take, because everybody wants to benefit from the deal.

Negotiation is an art which requires some qualities and skills and the following tips will help you develop them.

1. Before negotiation, know the objective, the goal, the purpose and the parties involved.
2. Anticipate few questions and their answers, the concession which can be offered and the best as well as the worst possible outcome.
3. Analyze your and the other party's strengths, weaknesses, bargaining power and negotiation techniques.
4. Analyze your BATANA i.e. Best Alternative to a Negotiated Agreement (Fisher and Urg, 1981, Getting To Yes, Hutchinson); It is a choice an individual makes. For example, If one is not comfortable with a particular negotiation, he can always refuse to accept it.
5. Carefully plan the structure of the negotiation, i.e. the opening, body and closing. These should be realistic and achievable.
6. Have a contingency plan.
7. Develop your inter-personal and non-verbal communication skills for effective negotiation.
8. Prioritize the issues which need immediate attention.
9. During negotiation, emphasize on a "win-win" situation which is beneficial to both the parties.
10. Concentrate on the problem and not the people involved.
11. Have a positive attitude, be co-operative, flexible and enthusiastic.
12. Don't lose your patience, stay calm, cool, confident, polite and have a professional approach.
13. Be a good and active listener.
14. Summarize the agreements/disagreements at regular intervals.

15. Focus on long term relationship rather than short term profit.
16. After negotiation, write the decisions taken and ensure that it signed by both the parties to avoid confusion and misunderstanding.

    Finally, I would conclude by the famous words of Wrigley and Moshe Dayan respectively.

    When two men in business always agree, one of them is unnecessary.

    If you want to make peace, you don't talk to your friends, you talk to your enemies.

## Rule 5: Discuss but never argue

Put forth your point in a very emphatic, positive and confident manner. Remember the 6 C's of effective communication: clarity, completeness, consciousness, confidence, correctness and courtesy.

Learn to disagree politely, if required. In fact, it is far better to put forward your point of view without specifically saying, "I disagree" or "You're wrong". Instead say, "I agree with you, but....", "We have heard many viewpoints but I would like to say...." Apply common sense to present your idea effectively.

A person who lacks leadership can't be a good teacher. The ability to show direction, co-ordination, inspiration, motivation, contribution at regular intervals, can make a positive impact on students.

However, the best scoring rounds are introduction, keeping the discussion on track, conclusion and listening skills.

An idea or a perspective which opens up new horizons and puts across new topics convincingly for discussion is always appreciated. Always strike a balance between expressing your ideas and listening to others. Conviction while speaking goes hand-in-hand with flexibility in approach and the ability to appreciate the viewpoint of other candidates.

*"The leaders who work most effectively, it seems to me, never say "I". And that's not because they have trained themselves not to say "I". They don't think "I". They think "we", they think "team". They understand their job is to make the team function. They accept responsibility and don't sidestep it, but "we" gets the credit. That is what creates trust, and enables you to get the task done."*

*– Peter Drucker.*

Finally, most of the discussions follow one of the 3 formats; structured, unstructured or specialized. Patience, perseverance, convincing power, self-confidence, ability to articulate one's thought and power of persuasion are the hallmarks of the winner in any discussion.

Strategies and suggestions for discussions:

- Knowledge is strength. A teacher with good reading habits has more chances to succeed.
- Pay attention to what and how to say.
- Be deliberate and slow in delivery of points.
- Follow the principle of politeness.
- Substantiate your point with suitable examples.
- Don't provide opportunities for others to talk, when you do.
- Be a good listener.
- Don't be loud, emotional or angry.
- Appreciate the viewpoints of others.
- Don't intervene unnecessarily when others speak.
- Make your comments short and crispy.
- Use simple, direct and straight forward language and avoid slang.
- Maintain rapport with fellow participants.
- When someone appreciates your point of view, respond positively and thank them for the compliments.
- Wind-up by incorporating all important points discussed and wind-up on time.

## Rule 6: Be a creator and not a slayer

Dale Carnegie, author of "How to win friends and influence people", once said, "You can make more friends in two months by becoming interested in other people, than you can in two years by trying to get people interested in you". Be a team player. No institution appreciates a greedy or lonely teacher. A good colleague is one with whom other colleagues would love to work with.

Be participative and polite. Share your views without enforcing them, maintain harmonious relationship, show respect, take interest in the institute's work, and show consideration by trying to understand your colleagues' point of view.

A good teacher sets realistic and attainable goals by developing a programme to involving all his subordinates in the goal setting process.

Being loyal, punctual, reliable, dependable and having earned a reputation of being honest and trustworthy, especially in crisis, are the great building blocks for success. Be kind, generous and positive. Praise positive qualities of others. Never commit anything if you can't do it. Fulfill all your promises. Be a giver, and not just a taker.

Don't ask anyone to lie for you. Remember that your body language portrays your self-confidence. The way a teacher carries himself/herself tells a story. Teachers with slumped shoulders and lethargic movements, display lack of self-confidence. They aren't enthusiastic about what they're doing as they don't consider themselves important.

By practicing good posture, you'll automatically feel more confident. Stand up straight, walk energetically, keep your head up, make eye contact and dress sharply. You'll make a positive impression on others and feel more and empowered.

### Count Your Blessings

I've never made a fortune,
and it's probably too late now.
But I don't worry about that much,
I'm happy anyhow.
And as I go along life's way,
I'm reaping better than I sowed.
I'm drinking from my saucer,
'Cause my cup has overflowed.
Haven't got a lot of riches,
and sometimes the going's tough.
But I've got loving ones all around me,
and that makes me rich enough.
I thank God for his blessings,
and the mercies He's bestowed.
I'm drinking from my saucer,
'Cause my cup has overflowed.
I remember times when things went wrong,
My faith wore somewhat thin.

But all at once the dark clouds broke,
and the sun peeped through again.
So Lord, help me not to gripe,
about the tough rows I have hoed.
I'm drinking from my saucer,
'Cause my cup has overflowed.
If God gives me strength and courage,
When the way grows steep and rough.
I'll not ask for other blessings,
I'm already blessed enough.
And may I never be too busy,
to help others bear their loads
Then I'll keep drinking from my saucer,
'Cause my cup has overflowed.
When I think of how many people
in this world have it worse than I do.
I realize just how blessed most of us really are.

\- William J. Henderson

## Rule 7: Appreciate individual differences

When we walk into a restaurant, we have so many options to choose from, each with a unique quality, very different from others. Similarly different individuals have different ideas, views, opinions, aptitude, curiosity and traits. Understand their disparities and respect them. Show your support by trying to overlook their

weaknesses and focus on their strengths. Cherish their positive qualities to overcome their weaknesses.

Never encourage unfair competition. Your action speaks louder than words. So never gossip about your colleague. Make sure you are using your ability for good and not for evil.

Stay away from greed, envy, resentment and annoyance. As rightly said by Barbara Bush, 'never lose sight of the fact that the most important yardstick of your success will be how you treat other people – your family, friends, and coworkers, and even strangers you meet along the way'. Just imagine individuals who consistently bring us down or demotivate us with their personal troubles and grumbles, do we want to be their friend for a long time? No. The same logic applies to our lives also. Be genuine and never try to build any false image about yourself.

Never try to change your colleagues (even though some contemporaries we meet are a little difficult to get along with) because they will not change unless they themselves want to change. All you can do is help them to accept change.

Realize the fact that there is no perfect boss. Self discipline is required for a healthy relationship. True commitment towards work can easily overcome all the hurdles.

Keep in mind the old Turkish saying that whoever seeks a friend without a fault remains without one. Develop a "forgive and forget" approach towards life. Treat others as you want others to treat you. This develop a positive work environment which can easily enhance an individual's productivity. On the contrary, a pessimist surrounding can easily demotivate us. Avoid lengthy discussions on problems you are having with your co-workers, seniors, juniors, parents, spouse or even children.

Factors like clarity, timeliness, conciseness, transparency, honesty, openness, scope for appropriate feedback and two way communication contribute to a good internal relationship.

## Rule 8: Be a very good listener

God gave us one mouth to do two jobs: eat and speak; but he gave us two ears to do just one job: listen. This indicates that Listening is more critical than speaking. Hence, it is necessary to improve the ability to listen through conscious efforts.

According to Dr. Sumita Chakraborty, "our blood pressure rises when we talk and rapidly drops when we listen. Hence, even from the point of view of maintaining good health, listening is better than speaking." Unfortunately, most of us are more used to talking than listening. Listening, she adds, requires patience, friendliness, openness, the desire to understand and observing non-verbal gestures.

Another study reveals that 45% of the total working hours in institutes are spent on listening, 30% are spent on speaking, 16% on reading and 9% on writing, in spite of which we listen at or below 25% efficiency rate, remember only about half of what's said during a 10 minute conversation and forget half of that within 48 hours. Hence, listening carefully and attentively is important.

Just listening doesn't mean you are going to act accordingly. Listen, assimilate, and then decide based on what you have heard and your own experience. Active listening involves hearing, understanding, concentrating and judgment.

Jiddu Krishnamurti once said, "When you're listening to somebody, completely and attentively, you're listening not only to the words, but also to the feeling of what is being conveyed, to the whole of it, not part of it". Effective listening, by its very nature, shows one's communication skill.

Finally, a glance at this checklist provided by Bovee, Thil and Schatzan in Business Communication Today to improve your listening skills:

**A) Look beyond the speaker's style.**

1. Don't judge the message by the speaker, but by the argument.
2. Ask yourself what the speaker knows that you don't.
3. Depersonalize your listening.
4. Decrease the emotional impact of what's being said.

**B) Fight distractions.**

1. Close doors.
2. Turn off radios or televisions.
3. Move closer to the speaker.
4. Stay ahead of the speaker by anticipating what will be said next and by summarizing what's already been said.
5. Don't interrupt – avoid sidetracking solutions and throwing the speaker off course.
6. Hold your rebuttal until you've heard the entire message.

**C) Provide feedback.**

1. Let the speaker know you're paying attention.
2. Maintain eye contact.
3. Offer appropriate facial expressions.
4. Paraphrase what you've heard when the speaker reaches a stopping point.
5. Keep all criticism and feedback positive.

**D) Listen actively.**

1. Listen for concepts, key ideas, and facts.
2. Be able to distinguish between evidence and argument, idea and example, fact and principle.

3. Analyze the key points, whether or not they are supported by facts.
4. Look for unspoken messages in the speaker's tone of voice.
5. Keep an open mind.
6. Ask questions that clarify.
7. Reserve judgment until the speaker has finished.
8. Take meaningful notes that are brief and to the point.

## Rule 9: Build your self-confidence

Jack Welch once said, "Confidence gives you courage and extends your reach. It lets you take greater risks and achieve far more than you ever thought possible". This powerfully conveys the enormous role self-confidence plays in achieving success in whatever you do.

Self confidence is a quality that everyone has a high regard for. Self confident teachers inspire confidence in others: their seniors, their subordinates, their juniors, their students and even their family and friends.

It is extremely important in almost every aspect of our lives and can be shown in many ways: our behaviour, attitude, body language, speaking skills and so on. Yet, so many people struggle to find it. Confidence gives immense strength to cope up with the negatives in our lives and empower ourselves.

Professor Raj Persaud conceives that true self confidence comes from an attitude where you promise yourself, no matter how difficult the problem life throws at you, that you will try as hard as you can to help yourself. You acknowledge that your efforts to help yourself resulting in success and being properly rewarded is not in your control.

Sadly, this can be a vicious circle. People who lack self-confidence can find it difficult to become successful and vice-versa. But, the good news is that it is not necessarily inherited. It can be learnt, developed and built and here are some steps you can take to do so.

- **Analyze your Strengths, Weaknesses, Opportunities and Threats (SWOT)** to set your goals: Think about what's important to you; where you really are and where you want to go. Dwell on your strengths, analyze and explore them. Set goals that utilize your strengths, curtail your weaknesses, apprehend your opportunities and direct your threats. Lack of confidence is not proportional to a person's abilities.

  In fact, there are people who are extremely talented and able, but lack confidence to show these abilities.

Walt Disney once said, "Somehow I can't believe that there are any heights that can't be scaled by a man who knows the secrets of making dreams come true. This special secret, it seems to me, can be summarized in four C's. They are curiosity, confidence, courage and consistency and the greatest of all is confidence. When you believe in a thing, believe in it all the way, implicitly and unquestionably".

Focus on what you have and not on what you don't have. Appreciate positives in other people. Be a leader and develop your leadership qualities. Go that extra mile for excellence. Set your goals and endure to achieve them.

- **Start managing your time:** Set realistic, systematic, purposeful, and attainable goals with a deadline. Try to arrange your schedule so that you will not have to hurry.

  Hurry, a blood brother to worry, helps shatter poise and self-confidence and contributes to fear and anxiety. Build the knowledge you need to succeed. Identify the skills you'll need to acquire and then look at how you can acquire these skills confidently.

## Decide your priorities

- What are your goals? (short as well as long term)
- How do you strive to achieve them? (Strategies/ blue print)
- When you want to reach that goal? (Deadline)
- What are your strengths and weaknesses? (SWOT analysis)
- Where do you want to see yourself 10 years down the line? (career aspirations)
- Why do you want to achieve your goal? (purpose)

- **Commit yourself to success:** Have a desire and become self-confident. It is an attitude characterized by a positive belief. Tell yourself, "I like things to take place and if they don't happen, I will make them happen." As Brian Tracy believed, with greater confidence in yourself and your abilities, you will set bigger goals, make bigger plans and commit yourself to achieving objectives that today you only dream about."

  Self confidence comes from not only setting high standards for you, but also continuously striving to achieve them. Overcome all your fears and suspicions calmly, logically and realistically.

- **Remember that your body language portrays your self-confidence:** The way a person carries himself/herself tells a story. Your posture displays your confidence. People with slumped shoulder and lethargic movements, display a lack of self-confidence. By practicing good posture, you'll automatically feel more confident.

- **Never be a defeatist:** Both low self confidence and over-confidence are unfavourable qualities. The best option is a balance between the two. Don't dwell on past failures because it will make you feel insignificant. Be less critical; become your own fan by cheering yourself all the time and tell yourself how great you are by looking at what you've already achieved. Sporadically, recall your past triumphs and achievements.

A self confident teacher easily accepts all complex challenges in his life and look at all setbacks as stepping stones to success. Never extol your own achievements/virtues or success, wait for others to do that. Accept compliments graciously.

Accept that nothing is perfect and the glass is half full and not half empty. "Without a humble but reasonable confidence in your own powers you cannot be successful or happy" – Norman Peale. Your acuity about yourself has tremendous impact on how others perceive you. Occasionally read motivational speeches of great leaders. Do what you believe is right. Be willing to take calculated risks.

- **Laugh and have fun:** Develop an "I can do" attitude. Smile even if there is no reason to smile. It will foster a sense of positivism that drives out negative thoughts. It is a two-edge sword. As Stacey Charter rightly said, "there comes a time when you have to stand up and shout: This is me! I look the way I look, think the way I think, feel the way I feel, love the way I am! I am a whole complex package. Take me....or leave me. Accept me or walk away! Do not try to make me feel like less of a person, just because I don't fit your idea of who I should be and don't try to change me to fit your mould. If I need to change, I alone will make that decision.

# How to be a Good Citizen?

## The Good Citizen

I am twenty one years old
And was raised in the proper way
To abide by the laws of land
And to live by the rules every day

I was raised to apply common sense
To any action I might make
And to use my own judgment
And not to fear making a mistake

I was raised to respect myself
And respect others at the same time
I was raised to respect the law
And not to resort to crime

I was raised to think for myself
And given the tools to do so
I was taught the right from wrong
And how to behave and how to say no

I loved my life and I was happy
I had a good job which paid very well
A large circle of great friends
And a shiny new car I called Annabel

So when I went to a party with friends
To celebrate a twenty first birthday

I drove them in my beloved Annabel
And drank only coke to my friends dismay

I remembered what I was taught
And I didn't drink and drive
Despite pressure from my peers
I made a conscious choice to stay alive

I had a good time at the party
And I was proud of myself for my stance
I had a good time at the party
Though friends teased me for my abstinence

All too soon the party ended
And we hugged and kissed our goodnights
Then we all went our separate ways
I got into Annabel and turned on the lights

I drove off safe in the knowledge
I had done the right thing staying dry
I observed all the speed restrictions
Not realizing I was soon about to die

I'm standing on the roadside
And see my broken body on the ground
Poor Annabel is smashed to pieces
With men in uniforms all around

A young man was led away in handcuffs
It seems he was a drunk driver
All his passengers were also dead
He was drunk and the only survivor

If he had been taught as I was
I would not now be lying dead
If he had been taught as I was
The road would not be coloured red

In my short life I was a good person
I was a good daughter to my parents
A good sister to my young brother
And good to my friends and conficents

There is so much I will now never do
My life will never be fulfilled
I was a good citizen until today
When through selfishness I was killed.

- Paul Curtis

## Rule 1: Identify your Ethical and Social Responsibility

Ethics is important not only in business, but in all aspects of life, because it is and the foundation on which any society is built. A business/society that lacks ethical principles is bound to fail sooner or later.

According to International Ethical Business Registry, there has been a dramatic increase in the ethical expectation of businesses and professionals over the past 10 years. Increasingly, customers, clients and employers are deliberately seeking out those who define the basic ground rules of their operations on a day-to-day basis.

Ethics refer to a code of conduct that guides an individual in dealing with others. Business ethics is a form of the art of applied ethics that examines ethical and moral problems that can arise in a business environment. It deals with issues regarding the moral and ethical rights, duties and corporate governance between a company and its shareholders, employees, customers, media, government, suppliers and dealers. It is the responsibility of a teacher not only to follow fair practices but also preach them. Henry Ford said that a business that makes nothing but money is a poor kind of business.

Ethics is related to all disciplines of an organization like accounting information, human resource management, sales and marketing, production, intellectual property, knowledge and skill, international business and economic system.

As said by Joe Paterno, success without honor is an unseasoned dish. It will satisfy your hunger, but won't taste good. In business world, the organization's culture sets standards for determining the difference between good and bad, right and wrong, fair and unfair.

"It is perfectly possible to make a decent living without compromising the integrity of the company or the individual", wrote business executive R. Holland, "Quite apart from the issues of rightness and wrongness, the fact is that ethical behaviour in business serves the individual and the enterprise in long run.", he added. And this principle has to be effectively followed by a teacher as a good teacher is an image of a good society.

Some management guru stressed that ethical organizations have an advantage over their competitors. "Consumers are used to buying products despite how they feel about the company that sells them", Said Cohen and Greenfield.

But a valued company earn a kind of customer loyalty most corporations only dream of as it appeals to its customers more than its product". "Price is what you pay. Value is what you get" – Warren Buffet. This belief has to be inculcated by a teacher in their students as they are the future of the nation.

Teachers have to remember that leading by example is the first step in fostering a culture of ethical behaviour in the institute. As rightly said by Robert Noyce, "if ethics are poor at the top, that behaviour is copied down through the organization. However the other methods include creating a common interest by favorable corporate culture, setting high standards, norms, framing attitudes for acceptable behaviour, making a written code of ethics applicable at all levels from top to bottom, deciding the policies of the institute.

Teachers and society are interdependent. Social responsibility is an ethical theory; a doctrine on how an entity, whether it is a government, corporation, organization or individuals has a responsibility towards society. It can be defined as the obligation of an individual to pursue those policies, to make those decisions or to follow those lines of actions which are desirable in terms of the objectives and values of his/her society.

As rightly said, It is better to be proactive towards a problem rather than reactive. One part of social responsibility is being responsible to people, for the actions of people and for actions that affect people. This demonstrates the obligation of a teacher towards different social groups. As Abraham Lincoln once said, public sentiment is everything. With public sentiment, nothing can fail, without it, nothing can succeed.

*A teacher needs to understand the utilitarian principle that says – Act in a way that results in the greatest good for the greatest number. The social responsibility concept is beneficial to the institute and the society. "The most significant contribution organized industry can make is by identifying itself with the life and the problems of the people, of the community to which it belongs, and by applying its resources, skills and talents to serve and help them"*

*- Late J. R. D. Tata.*

Every teacher must have a code of conduct which directs human behaviour determe universal rules and laws of behaviour.

Social responsibility is voluntary. It is about going beyond the legal responsibility. It cannot be imposed by law and thus, it needs willful acceptance and self discipline. According to renowned Indian Jurist Nani Palkivala, "What is the point in having laws and laws upon laws if your inner consciousness is not there, which enables you to do right things for a right conclusion?"

In other words, if you expect fairness and justice all around, it has to be found within the heart of businessmen. If the ethical sense dies in the heart of businessmen, no constitutions, no law, no court can save it. It is only within yourself that you have to find the ideals you are struggling to establish.

There are many ways through which we can help to make this world a better place to live. They are as follows.

## Rule 2: Be a good human being

- There are ample number people around us who need our help. Your little help can make a big difference in their lives. So, dynamically contribute for the welfare of the society.
- Listen and appreciate the point of view of others.
- Don't damage your surroundings. Throw your garbage in the dustbin, and never infuriate your neighbours. Maintain a good relationship with your neighbours, colleagues, friends etc. Never play politics and be pleasant.
- Participate in society meeting and share your ideas.
- Don't damage national property.
- Show empathy and respect for others. Be considerate and caring to people who can't help themselves.
- Follow the speed limit while driving. Never drink and drive and if you find someone drunk at a party, try to drive them home or book a cab for them.
- Love your nation. As Theodore Roosevelt said, the first requisite of a good citizen in this republic of ours is that he shall be able and willing to pull his weight. Support local trade and business which will lessen our dependency on foreign products and will preserve our currency.
- Stay away from drugs, alcohol and bad influences.

## Rule 3: Respect your ideals, doctrines and moral codes

- Follow the laws and orders of the nation. Try to be well mannered. Education is often considered as a requirement for a good citizenship and it helps them to take fair and firm decisions.
- Fulfill your responsibility by voting and participating in the political system. If you don't vote, you have no authority criticize the government. George Jean Nathan once said that bad officials are elected by good citizens who do not vote. Encourage people to give their valuable vote.
- You must know what is going on in politics. You can do that by reading newspapers, magazines or watching news channels. Get involved in all the political happenings of the country. Understand your judiciary system and its functioning. Egg on ideas, suggestions for country's growth and development.
- Participate in donating blood, helping NGO's cleanliness devices, preserving our national heritage, planting trees, regularly singing the national anthem and supporting democracy.
- Pay taxes on time.
- Help your society to raise money for any charity. You can join an organization that supports orphans, senior citizens, disabled or someone affected by natural calamities.
- Never spread rumours, especially in crisis.

## Rule 4: Be a role model for your child

- Teach your child to be sincere, chivalrous and thoughtful.
- A good teacher creates a positive influence at home and in the institute which is beneficial to the society at large.
- In any house where the parents follow the law, you will find their children to be direct and open. Honesty and sincerity will always flow from top to bottom. Create a positive, law abiding environment.
- Teach them to go that extra mile for their country. Celebrate your country's success with your family, friends and neighbours.
- Respect regional and cultural differences of your nation and educate your child to do the same.
- Use recycled products and persuade your family to do the same.
- Support afforestation, which will help to make the air healthy, pure and safe.
- Salute your national flag and explain its importance to your child.
- To inculcate patriotic feeling among your child, tell them the stories and anecdotes of our great national heroes who have sacrificed their lives to make our country independent. (It is necessary for you to understand our national history).
- Coach them about their duties and responsibilities as a citizen of a democratic nation.

Thus in a nutshell, I would conclude by the words of Francis Duggan.

When I hear someone referred to as a good citizen I feel like laughing aloud
Your government approves of you; big brother of you proud
But if you die tomorrow the government won't care
To them you are just a number and your type are not rare,
The government and big brother you do not need to impress
Their approval or disapproval will not ease your cares and stress
The one who is a good friend to the neighbour is surely far more great
Than the one big brother looks upon as a good friend of the State,
The good citizens pay their taxes and work hard for their pay
And they vote in a lousy Government on National election day
And good citizens dob in their fellow citizen
to the police for a minor traffic offence
In their quest for big brother's approval they sacrifice common sense
And many more good citizens they passed away today
They worked hard and voted in a lousy government and their taxes they did pay.

# How to Please your Seniors

## Decree 1: Be accountable

*"Act as if what you do makes a difference. It does"*
*– William James.*

Be loyal, committed and dedicated to your institute. Accept responsibilities sincerely. Know exactly what is expected of you and ensure that you do exactly the same. Seek feedback on your performance. If any problem arises, just don't immediately go to your senior to fix it. Understand the fact that problems are an inevitable part of any work life. So, face them with conviction and courage. Try to find solutions to your problems and solve them yourself.

Be a problem solver. At times, you can't take decisions to address the problems, but you can definitely suggest measures to your seniors to fix them. Whenever you approach your seniors for any problem, be ready with few alternative solutions and your preferred solution to overcome that problem. Avoid complaining about the situation.

If due to any reasons you are unable to finish your syllabus on time, try to give valid reasons. Repeatedly do more than what is expected from you. Seniors always admire those employees who perform their task properly and do more than what is expected of them. As rightly said by Theodore Roosevelt, far and away the best prize that life offers is the chance to work hard at something worth doing. Try to meet your deadlines and finish your task. Work extra hours when you want to meet your deadlines. Always follow your institute's rules and principles. Never try to breach them.

## Decree 2: Your body language speaks for you

*"Body language is a very powerful tool. We had body language before we had speech, and apparently, 80% of what you understand in a conversation is read through the body, not the words."*
*– Deborah Bull*

Body language is non-verbal communication. It usually complements our verbal communication. Your gestures, postures, eye-contact, body movement convey your attitude. Follow a proper dress code. Understand the body language of your seniors as well. Small things like sitting up straight, maintaining eye contact, walking enthusiastically can help you get noticed. Your seniors may judge you by your body language, so maintain a tranquil posture.

Many researchers have revealed that your seniors give more importance to how an employee reacts through body language than spoken words. Your seniors can easily evaluate your wit and capabilities with your style of walking, posture, facial expressions, and manner of talking as your body language may be a sign of your anger, courtesy, politeness, ennui etc. It can convey whether you are happy, content, unsatisfied, confused or even de-motivated. Your body reflects your confidence and demonstrates whether you are controlled, relaxed, primed, apprehensive or unprepared. So make sure that you use non-verbal communication as an influential tool that smoothers your communication. Even if you are in some tension or trauma, never reveal it through your body language.

## Decree 3: Be calm. Be cool.

*"History has demonstrated that the most notable winners usually encountered heartbreaking obstacles before they triumphed. They won because they refused to become discouraged by their defeats"*

*– B. C. Forbes.*

In any crisis, be calm and composed. You have the power to control your own emotions. So make the right choice. This will make you reliable, trustworthy and someone your seniors can readily depend on. Don't fight over petty issues with your colleagues or your seniors. Internal rivalry means a waste of talent and resources. Ignore employees who add stress to your life. Never let them bring you down. If they are impolite, patiently address their issues. Try to be surrounded by people who are unruffled and who will cherish and foster you. As David Mallet once said, affliction is the wholesome soil of virtue, where patience, honor, sweet humility, and calm fortitude, take root and strongly flourish. Find some place in your institute (whether common room, library, gym) where you can sit alone for some time and relax.

Develop a good sense of humour. Study has found that individuals who have a good sense of humour can easily deal with their pain, frustration and hassles. It also increases your resistance power and is an imperative ingredient for a hale, hearty and blissful life.

Here are few ways to augment your sense of humor:-

- Discern what your seniors find humorous.
- Watch movies that are hilarious.
- See the comical side of complicated or thwarting situation.

## Decree 4: Be dependable

*"Each man is questioned by life; and he can only answer to life by answering for his own life; to life he can only respond by being responsible."*
*– Viktor E. Frankly.*

In today's competitive world, satisfying your seniors is challenging. Be sincere and loyal so that your seniors can easily rely on you. Show dedication to your job and your institute. Be proud to be associated with your institute. Avoid being late at work especially for any meeting. Try to arrive before your seniors. Never keep them waiting. Be prepared for the meeting by knowing the agenda beforehand. Do your homework. Avoid being absent without prior intimation.

If due to some lecture or any other administrative task, you can't attend any meeting, inform your seniors about it before the meeting. Never try to object their proposals instantaneously in any meeting, conference or discussions. In fact, try to explain to them the difficulties one might face while executing the idea. Never mention their mistakes directly to their seniors. Ross Perot remarked that something in human nature causes us to slack off at our moment of greatest accomplishment. As you become successful, you will need a great deal of self-discipline, sense of balance, humility, and commitment.

Never lie. Your seniors are more experienced than you. If you're caught, you will lose your trustworthiness or even your job. Never discuss your institute's problems, internal politics or policies with any outsider who can tarnish the goodwill of the institute as well as your reputation.

## Decree 5: Raise your efficiency

*"Efficiency is doing things right; effectiveness is doing the right things."*
*– Peter F. Drucker.*

It is difficult to float above mediocrity and impress your seniors. But if you want to stand out from the crowd, raise your efficiency and effectiveness. Never play politics. Abstain from internal politics. By no means, be a part of institute conflicts. Don't hesitate to ask for help from your seniors. As pointed out by Henry C. Link, while one person hesitates because he feels inferior, the other is busy making mistakes and becoming superior.

Try to gain a competitive edge (through your hard work/ positive attitude/ enthusiasm/ knowledge or any other factor) and your seniors they will always appreciate it. Don't always say "yes", "agreed" to all ideas and suggestions. If you disagree with something, politely try to convey to them your viewpoint. Be ready to speak your mind.

Suggest creative ideas that will enhance the productivity, reduce the time and cost for the institute and reduce duplication of work. Avoid grammatical errors while drafting any letter. Be very good in your subject. Build a strong relationship with your seniors by encouraging a two way healthy communication. Learn from their experiences and expertise. Complete your work on time. If you finish your syllabus or any other administrative task assigned to you, let them know about it and then move on to the next assignment.

## Decree 6: Develop a forgive and forget approach

*"To forgive is the highest, most beautiful form of love. In return, you will receive untold peace and happiness."*

*– Robert Muller*

If you have a fight with your colleagues, don't hold a grudge for long as it carries a negative image within the institute. Never take their behaviour personally. Try to forget mistakes of your colleagues and juniors. Have you ever evaluated why forgiveness is difficult:-

- Is it since we are hesitant to permit the exit of our ego?
- Or due to our resentment.
- Or because they haven't expressed regret.
- Or we covet to chastise or impair the offenders.

But forgiving and forgetting is mutually beneficial. It aids to decrease your worry, annoyance, acrimony, antipathy, gloominess and other depressing sentiments. One study established a connection between forgiving someone for their disloyalty/ unfaithfulness and enhancement in blood pressure, heart rate. Louise Hay stated that we may not know how to forgive, and we may not want to forgive; but the very fact that we are willing to forgive begins the healing process. If due to any reason your relationship with your senior is spoilt, ensure that you are the one who takes an initiative to mend it and recover the damage by identifying the root cause of the problem.

## Decree 7: Gossip. Stay away from it

*"Who gossips to you will gossip about you"*

*– Turkish proverb.*

Don't be a gossiper. Don't encourage rumours within or outside the institute. It will needlessly drain your time and energy. Learn to keep quiet and not to pass any comments on institute's internal politics.

Assess each statement as to whether it reveals the positives of your seniors and you or does it focus just on their mistakes or blunders. If it is the latter case, never share it with anyone. In any institution, false rumours and information spreads like a forest fire because it seems to more fascinating and appealing.

Be a diplomat. Never waste your institute's time and other resources in any unconstructive task. As supposed by Dr Seymour Epstein, super achievers don't waste time in unproductive, esoteric, or catastrophic thoughts They think constructively and they know that their level of thinking determines their success. Always speak the truth. Be good to everyone and say good things about everyone. Be professional all the time. Here are few rules to remember to stay away from gossiping.

- Identify whether the news is really imperative? If not, then focus on your personal development.
- Don't be an initiator who spreads rumours.
- Even if you hear something, change the topic; leave that place (say you have something important to do); or as a last alternative you can even express your displeasure talking about that matter.
- Stay impartial. If someone gossips with you, they will definitely gossip about you.

## Decree 8: Hard work really pays

*"A dream doesn't become reality through magic; it takes sweat, determination and hard work."*

*– Colin Powell.*

If you perform your task smoothly, it will make life simpler and allow you to concentrate on the bigger goals. Keep a record of all your work. As James A. Garfield once said, if the power to do hard work is not a skill, it's the best possible substitute for it. Be a quick learner. Learn to do things that aren't easy or that are denied by everyone else. It will help you to learn something new and improve your knowledge. Try to search for new developments in your subject which requires lots of reading. Write few research articles on your subject.

Adopt the work culture of your institute. as it can enhance your approach to work. Don't consider any task as inferior, perform them with full commitment and devotion. Perfection is a gradual process. So gradually develop that skill and do your best every time.

Most of your colleagues will do what's simplest and shun tje rest. If you want to stand out of the crowd, accept difficult challenges as an unusual prospect and you will find that in long run, you will compete with yourself. Always remember that difficult challenges lead to better outcomes. You have to acknowledge the affect that the road to success requires a lot of hard work. Your career will reach new heights if you truly work hard.

## Decree 9: Learn the art of handling interviews

In today's scenario, from the time a person seeks appointment in an organization, till the time he leaves his employers, interviews happen in his career path. An interview reveals the views, ideas, and attitudes of the interviewee as well as the skills of the interviewer.

The objective is to gather details and relevant information by talking to the interviewee and thereafter making an assessment, appraisal or evaluation about the suitability of the candidate for the offer or position available. It is always goal oriented, and is of different types which could be conducted for variety of purposes like selection, promotion, exit, grievances, orientation, admission, appraisal etc.

The candidate must be very clear about the purpose of the event which is to persuade the employer that he has the skill, background and ability to do the job and he can comfortably fit into the institute. The candidate has to be well prepared for questions on his resume, area of interest, his strengths, weaknesses, his present position, the position he applied for, the nature of organization, its history, current activities etc... his knowledge on all such questions will impress the interviewer. Keep your resume current, focussed and free from error. Attach a cover letter along to create a good impression and build on your conventional skills so that you may not be at a loss for words while replying to questions posed by the interviewer.

From the moment you enter the interview room, till the time you leave it, you will be under constant scrutiny. Everybody appreciates a presentable personality. Be punctual, well groomed, clean and get insights into what the company expects from the employees. Cut and clean your nails, wear well ironed clothes, comb your hair properly, Resist the temptation to wear perfume, bright colours, loud nail polish and cover up the tattoos.

The posture, body language, gestures, oral delivery, eye contact is of great relevance as it gives positive impression about the candidate. A firm handshake, a pleasant natural smile and a brief exchange of words is sufficient to break the ice in the beginning. In a lunch interview, eat slowly, never speak with food in mouth, focus your attention on the conversation rather than your food and refrain from ordering messy food. Finally after the interview, a follow-up letter in a positive tone is an essential tool.

Here are few questions whose answers can be practiced in advance.

1. Tell us something about yourself?
2. Why should we employ you?
3. What are your strengths and weaknesses?
4. Why did you leave your last job?
5. What experience do you have in this field?

6. Where do you see yourself in 2-5 years?
7. What do you know about this institute?
8. Why do you want to work for this institute?
9. What have you done to improve your knowledge last year?
10. Who is your role model and why?
11. What contributions could you make in this institute that would help you to stand out from other applicants?
12. Do you consider yourself successful?

**Interview Tips**

- Know the time, date and location of the interview.
- Get your certificates, references ready before date.
- Check before entering whether your mobile phone is on silent mode or switched off.
- Express your strengths but don't over-communicate.
- Brevity is the soul of the wit, i.e. employ simple and fairly known language.
- Never try to camouflage by bluffing.
- Stick to your self-worth.
- Be an active listener.
- Maintain eye contact throughout the interview.
- Practice positive visualization.
- Rehearse your interview.
- Never try to be funny.
- Never lie. As rightly said by Mark Twain, "If you tell the truth, you never have to remember anything."
- Avoid criticism of the previous employer, never blame others.
- Maintain calmness and be positive.
- Avoid nervousness or down heartedness in the interview room.
- Never keep your hands or any of your belongings on the table.
- Don't argue.
- If they are asking you embarrassing or confusing questions, let them check your temperament and don't allow your confidence to shatter.
- At the end, ask any question to seek clarification regarding the institute profile, service, condition etc.
- Don't forget to thank the interviewer for having spared time for you.

## Decree 10: Join some cell or committee within your institute

*"In order that people may be happy in their work, these three things are needed: They must be fit for it: They must not do too much of it: And they must have a sense of success in it."*

*– John Ruskin.*

Never be the run-of-the-mill tiresome teacher. Volunteer your time and energy in some co-curricular or extracurricular activities. By joining some cell, you might feel trapped, jaded, aggravated or even over fraught but accept it as a new escapade. It will help you in number of ways.

- To recognize new potentials and to discover your talent.
- It allows you to come out of your comfort zone.
- To boost your self-belief.
- To increase your endurance and tolerance.
- It demonstrates true consideration for your students.
- To gain immense satisfaction.
- To analyze different perspectives of the same situation.
- It raises your willingness to help students achieve their personal goals/ targets.
- To change your beliefs about what you can't do.
- To learn new skills. "Wherever we are and whatever we are doing, it is possible to learn something that can enrich our lives and the lives of others... No one's education is ever complete."-Sir. John Templeton
- To offer help to someone else. (Especially your students).
- It gives you a chance to socialize with others.

## Decree 11: Know your subject well

*"It is the supreme art of the teacher to awaken joy in creative expression and knowledge."*

*– Albert Einstein*

With an immense pressure to increase revenue, cut cost and improve result forecast, companies are demanding that their employees should generate more revenue, acquire more and bigger global accounts and more "A" grade clients, for which they require effectual human resources who possess passable knowledge in management techniques and strategy to achieve targets.

Highly motivated, experienced and qualified teachers can play a big role in creating such employees for the corporate world by nurturing their students and providing them the required information, facts, figures, explanation or skills during their academic phase and teaching them to be flexible to adopt themselves to their organizational culture. Teacher comprehension is an important attribute of student learning. There can be a direct effect of the teachers' academic and professional skills on student's performance. As John F. Kennedy rightly said, the goal of education is the advancement of knowledge and the dissemination of truth.

So be familiar with all the information you need to teach your subject. It should be a proper combination of theory as well as practical. It can be couched (acquired through experience or expertise) or overt (gained through abstract understanding of your subject). Knowledge of subject content, general acquaintances, information of related areas is very essential for any teacher. So, be well acquainted with your subject and believe me, your seniors will always treasure you.

## Decree 12: Listen thoughtfully

*"The most basic of all human needs is the need to understand and be understood. The best way to understand people is to listen to them."*
*– Ralph Nichols*

Be an attentive and keen listener. Dedicatedly listen to the expectation of your senior and ensure that you follow every minute detail. This will help you to achieve your targets faster. Effective listeners remember that words have no meaning - people have meaning. "The assignment of meaning to a term is an internal process; meaning comes from inside us. And although our experiences, knowledge and attitudes differ, we often misinterpret each other's messages while under the illusion that a common understanding has been achieved." - Larry Barker.

As discussed previously, listening is a dynamic process that involves hearing, understanding and reviewing. In a nutshell, here are a few tips for being a good listener, details are conferred in the previous chapter.

a) Listen attentively.

b) Be focused.

c) Let the speaker finish first.

d) Understand the core idea of the speaker.

e) If you don't understand anything, ask again.

f) Give appropriate feedback whether you have understood the expectations of seniors or not. If yes, proceed with your conversation. If no, ask again.

## Decree 13: Good manners are very important

*"I have a respect for manners as such, they are a way of dealing with people you don't agree with or like"*
*– Margaret Mead.*

Practice good hygiene. It might seem simple and unstated but ignoring cleanliness can create a poor impression. As Emily Post said, "Manners are a sensitive awareness of the feelings of others. If you have that awareness, you have good manners, no matter what fork you use". Keep up good stance even while eating.

While talking on mobile phone try to keep your voice minimum. Keep your cubicle/ desk neat, organized and clean.

Good manners demonstrate your reverence, concern and contemplation and help to build healthier associations with your seniors. Here are few manners to practice.

- Never speak loudly.
- While communicating with your juniors, don't be arrogant and impolite.
- Don't talk only about yourself or your family/ friends.
- Respect your elders, even if they are your juniors, you can learn ample from them.
- Use words like "thank-you", "you're welcome", "please", "I am sorry". Never use words like "yeah", "hhmmm", "naa", "oops", and "aahh" repetitively.
- Never use grimy language or crack childish jokes. Your seniors may treat you as immature. To impress them, use civilized language.
- Don't interrupt others while they are speaking.
- Unless in emergency, never call your seniors after work hours.
- Never write letters or notes with red pen.
- Use a dictionary or the computer's spell check while writing any letter, e-mail or notes to your senior if you are uncertain about your grammar or spellings.
- Never use SMS language like "2" instead of "to" or "u" in place of "you", "v" as a substitute of "we" and so on.
- Don't purposely humiliate others.

## Decree 14: Never underestimate planning

*Planning is a critical tool. The Pareto Principle say's that 80% of job is completed in 20% of time. Another application in a non-planning environment is that 80% of the efforts tend to achieve only 20% of the results. By thinking and planning we can reverse this to 20% of the efforts achieving 80% of the results. This signifies the importance of planning. "A plan is a trap laid to capture the future"*

*– Allen.*

Planning is the process by which you determine whether you should attempt the task, work out the most effective way of reaching your target and prepare to overcome unexpected difficulties with adequate resources as they help to achieve the maximum effects from given efforts.

It bridges the gap from where you are to where you want to be. It provides a framework within which we must operate. It is a proactive process that is intended to help individuals, group and organization's performance objective. But people avoid planning because of organizational problems (poor effort and reward structures, "the get-stuck in" culture, no monetary/ non monetary motivation) or individual problems (laziness, lack of commitment, resistance to change, fear of failure, no experience).

An ideal plan should be simple, clear, suitable, flexible, continuous, comprehensive, complete, realistic, acceptable and balanced with clear unity of purpose and direction. It offers a benchmark against which actual performance can be measured and reviewed. A plan can avoid mistakes and recognize hidden opportunities.

It helps us to understand more clearly what we want to achieve, when we can do it and how we should do it in a logical order. As rightly said by Thomas A. Edison, being busy doesn't always mean real work. The objective of all work is production or accomplishment and to either of these ends, there must be forethought, system, planning, intelligence and honest purpose, as well as perspiration. Seeming to do is nothing.

A plan should be a realistic view of expectation, depending upon the activities, a plan can be long range, intermediate and of short range. Always set practical targets/ deadlines. Plans should be pragmatic, which means that you should know what you are capable of and what is expected of you by your superiors. It is a blue-print of business growth and a road map of development.

It is looking ahead with a defined goal in writing which is realistic, specific, acceptable and easily measurable. Remember, the plan will not solve all your problems. Planning is not a magic pill to cure all ails. It is just one of the vital ingredients needed for success.

Proper planning enables you to turn your dreams into reality. Failing to plan to win is the same as planning to lose. If you fail to plan, you plan to fail. Planning is a process that involves making and evaluating interrelated decisions.

It is the selection of your mission, objectives, values, beliefs and translation of knowledge into action. Dwight D. Eisenhower once said, that plans are nothing, planning is everything. A good planner takes into account all the internal factors (new syllabus, services or requirement of the institute, new technology, changes in organizational structure, changes in the vision, values, norms) and external factors (competition, social, economic, global, demographic, natural, technological, task, political, legal), makes good assumptions about the environment, analyses them and focus on the critical ones.

Planning is an anticipatory decision making process that involves situational analysis, forecasting outcomes and events, considering implementation issues and contingencies. "Planning is bringing the future into the present so that you can do something about it now" – Alan Lakein. Planning is not guesswork, it is a conscious determination based on objectives and involves choosing among alternatives. It is an ongoing process that prevents small problems from becoming big.

In daily life, spend 10-15 minutes at the beginning of each day planning for the day or the next day. It will help you to schedule your tasks, organise yourself, ensures unity in decision making, change management, stability and provide solution to problems. Keep some spare time too, as unexpected situations may arise.

Finally, I remember the famous words of Tim Driskell, a renowned ice climber, to all those who wished to climb "Unexpected things can and do happen. Be Prepared. Expect the unexpected. Plan for the worst; but hope for the best!"

Here are some important ways to effective planning.

- "Planning is an intellectual process, conscious determination of courses of action, the basis of decision on purpose, facts and considered estimates."
  – Koontz and O'Donnell.
- Create a culture within the institute that is open to planning.
- Focus the plan on goals.
- Be aware of all the changes that need to be made.
- Gather all the resources needed.
- Make a brief SWOT (Strengths, Weaknesses, Opportunities and Threats) analysis.
- Have a contingency plan.

## Decree 15: Be an optimist

*"One of the things I learned the hard way was that it doesn't pay to get discouraged. Keeping busy and making optimism a way of life can restore your faith in yourself."*
*– Lucille Ball*

Be positive; keep an affirmative attitude at work. Ask yourself the following questions.

- What is your personal goal?
- What are your institutional objectives?
- What do your seniors want you to accomplish?
- Is it in line with your personal objectives?

As mentioned by Robert Conroy, one must cultivate optimism by committing themselves to a cause, a plan or a value system. They'll feel that they are growing in a meaningful direction which will help them rise above day-to-day setbacks.

Once you answer all the questions, you can easily draft your plans to achieve your institute's, as well as your personal objectives. Make your institute's objectives your personal priority. Ally your professional growth with the institute's objectives and you will find your seniors support in achieving your goals. Your positive attitude will make it more difficult for others to give you angst and pain.

## Decree 16: Learn punctuality and time management skills

*"Time = life; therefore, waste your time and waste your life, or master your time and master your life."*
*– Alan Lakein.*

If you start any project, ensure that you try to complete the same before the deadline. Never try to overload yourself by accepting more work than you can handle as it may result in decline in efficiency. Commit only when you can deliver on time. One of the reasons of stress and de-motivation is overcommitment of the employees. Failing to meet the expectations can result in low self esteem and unhappiness. If you are overloaded with work, solicit your seniors for help.

Identify where you often waste most of the time, try to change your habits around these activities. Wasting time is an indicator of poor management skills. "Determine never to be idle. No such person will have occasion to complain of the want of time, who never loses any. It is wonderful how much can be done if we are always doing."- Thomas Jefferson. Find out whether your seniors regard 5-10 minutes late as a tolerable extent of regularity. If yes, you are lucky. If no, try as hard as you can to always be punctual. If you don't come on time, they may think it as an insult to disregard others' precious time. Thrust yourself to reach at least 15 minutes before time for everything.

## Decree 17: Avoid asking too many questions

*"You don't want a million answers as much as you want a few forever questions. The questions are diamonds you hold in the light. Study a lifetime and you see different colours from the same jewel. The same questions, asked again, bring you just the answers you need, just the minute you need them."*

*– Richard Bach*

Sometimes, asking questions is vital to perform proficiently and to keep your relationship strong with your seniors. However, asking the same questions can be aggravating. Due to your inquisitiveness, you may unknowingly ask too many questions, but ensure that you don't ask the same questions again and again. The best conversation is the one that will allow your seniors to be a part of the dialogue without feeling grilled. As Lee J. Colan stated, ask the right questions.

Make sure that your question is succinct and rational. Don't ask superfluous questions. Never ask too many personal/irrelevant questions. It's none of your business. Don't just ask questions to make conversation. In fact, bad questions can destroy the discussion and convert it into very dull and boring talk. If you ask many questions, one after the other, your seniors may consider you as a time sucker, and if they get exhausted and annoyed, they may try to avoid you.

## Decree 18: Discover the art of resume writing

Your Curriculum Vitae (CV) is the first impression that portrays your image. A CV, also known as resume, personal profile, bio-data or summary is a written statement of an individual's personal history – educational qualifications, work-experience, achievements, biographical details, references etc. that makes an individual suitable for getting selected for a job and is usually attached to an application letter. Its core objective is to convince the interviewer that you are the perfect candidate for the position. The key elements are contents, focus, uniqueness, structure and design. Visually, the CV should be unique, attractive, easy to read, tailor made, one of its kind, almost unmatched and specifically written in terms of job requirement.

Following are some important categories of information in the Resume:

1. **Personal Details/ Data :-** Include your name, address, contact number, e-mail address, mother tongue, other languages known, strengths, career objectives, interest / hobbies (never intend to list watching t.V. reading magazines as your hobbies). Applications for overseas should include nationality, passport number and foreign languages known.
2. **Educational Qualifications :-** Include all details of institutions attended, degrees/ diplomas obtained, scores obtained, name of the examination body/ university, special subjects/ specialization (if any); future information which can be added as awards, prizes, scholarship received, participation in co-curricular sports/ cultural activities/ projects. List your qualification in order of your relevance, i.e. from most to least important.
3. **Work Experience :-** Include the institute's name, position held, period of time, tenure of service, job description, job specfications and any other achievements. Qualify your experiences; show you're result oriented by connecting your skills with job history. Any experience that highlights your skills or showcase your achievements can be included. Highlight any goals which you achieved ahead of time. Remember: never write "no experience". Instead, write "fresh graduate".
4. **References :-** Educational, Professional and Character references are supplied for verification of facts which one has presented on the Resume. As a rule, don't include references in your CV, keep them ready but provide only if asked.

Omit all needless information like social security number, marital status, health, citizenship, age, irrelevant awards/ association/ membership/ publication/ recreation activities/ references and travel history. A resume should be simple, clean, very easy to read, symmetrical, balanced and uncrowded, since it is a tool with one specific purpose - to win an interview and make an effective impression on your employer. Here are few significant tips for resume writing.

**DO'S**

- Keep it brief and concise. Shorter is usually better.
- Highlight your strengths and de-emphasize your weaknesses.
- Italics, alignment, boldface, bulleting, underlining and font size should all be similar throughout the resume.
- Check your resume for proper grammar and correct spelling.
- Whenever you feel that a particular facet or characteristic might work to your disadvantage, delete it immediately.
- Proofread and have an expert review your resume, avoid typographical errors.
- Take a laser printout of the CV on plain, white paper. Handwriting, typing, dot matrix printing and even ink jet printing looks unprofessional.
- Finally, be honest; never lie since it can be checked for its verity anytime in the future.

**DON'TS**

- Use long winded sentences and old fashioned language.
- Use "I", "me", "my" in the CV. Sprinkle your CV with personal pronouns.
- Overuse professional jargons and abbreviations.
- Enclose supporting documents unless they are asked for.
- Fold or roll the resume.
- Go into reasons for leaving any of your previous jobs.
- Mention previous pay rates, supervisors name and designation, second mailing address, i.e. your permanent address.

## Decree 19: Do SWOT analysis of yourself and your seniors

*"If one advances confidently in the direction of his dreams,*
*and endeavours to live the life which he has imagined,*
*he will meet with a success unexpected in common hours."*
*– Henry David Thoreau*

Understand and realize the strengths of your seniors and your institute and focus on them. Accept their limitations and appreciate their strong points. As believed by Helen Keller, no pessimist ever discovered the secrets of stars, or sailed to an uncharted land, or opened a new heaven to the human spirit. Try to find answer to the following questions.

- Is your senior ambitious?
- Are you more ambitious than him?

- What is the best motivating factor for him (money or appreciation)?
- Are his personal goals in tune with the institute's objectives?
- Is he an idealist?
- Is he a team player?
- Does he encourage his team?

Once you evaluate all the above questions, you can easily identify his potency and flaws. Analyze various factors like institute's policies, senior's frame of mind, your junior's efficiency, previous success/ failures, past records etc before giving any suggestions. Anticipate your superior's needs and expectations and fulfill them by following proper orders. Focus on positives rather than on negatives; substitute your disparagement with the support for your seniors.

In addition to your seniors' analysis, you will definitely succeed in life if you use your strengths to the optimum level and reduce your weaknesses. If you analyze your personal potency, you can easily realize plenty of opportunities and by assessing your limitation, you can easily reduce the threats.

## Decree 20: Be a team player

*"The way a team plays as a whole determines its success. You may have the greatest bunch of individual stars in the world, but if they don't play together, the club won't be worth a dime."*

*– Babe Ruth*

Craft an affable work milieu when you encourage and support your colleagues and juniors. Be respectful, gracious and well-mannered with them. Trust them, show respect and consideration. Try to understand their mood and anger. Set high standards for yourself as well as for others. Help them to achieve their personal goals. Give authentic accolades to your seniors if they have done something good for you. Compliment them for their efforts and success, but ensure that the compliment is genuine and not just flattery. Never show that you are jealous of their success. Accept your differences.

Bill Bradley rightly explained team player as the one who respects his fellow human being, treat them fairly, disagree with them honestly, enjoy their friendship, explore your thoughts about one another candidly, work together for a common goal and help one another achieve it.

In any institute, pleasant and healthy rapport between a senior and his employees is very important. Give credit to others if they really deserve it. Reward and appreciate them for their success. Show your seniors that you give importance to your coworker's suggestion by appreciating their views. Celebrate your institute's success. Try to remember their birthdays or anniversaries and greet them on those days. Never make faulty excuses or blame other team members for your failures, since it may create a negative impact on your seniors.

## Decree 21: Update your skills and knowledge

*No matter what your product is, you are ultimately in the education business. Your customers need to be constantly educated about the many advantages of doing business with you, trained to use your products more effectively, and taught how to make never-ending improvement in their lives.*

*- Robert G Allen.*

Try to learn more and enhance your skills. Find out from different sources about the skills you need in performing your task and try to achieve those competencies which can also help you in job enrichment. This will make you more valuable in the institute and increase your growth opportunities. Inculcate special reading habits, especially of your subject, to be ahead of the game. Plan in advance how you will use that knowledge for the betterment of students and institute.

Be innovative and encourage creativity. Charles Darwin said, "accept change as part of your life. It is neither the strongest of the species that survive, nor the most intelligent, but the one most responsive to change". Update yourself with the latest technical modernization and international developments Attend various seminars that update your knowledge and to know the current trends in your subject. Try to use them for your students and institute. Understand their expectation as well. Seek out all the relevant information you need to perform your task efficiently.

## Decree 22: Be firm on your values and principles

*"A person that values its privileges above its principles soon loses both."*

*- Dwight D. Eisenhower.*

All employers respect an honest teacher. It also helps to increase student's confidence for any teacher. Set an example for your juniors. Here are my 15 guiding values and principles:

- Develop your colleagues and look out for their wellbeing.
- Faith in your institute's policies.
- Confidence on your seniors.
- Admiration for personal traits of any employee.
- Trust of seniors on you in sharing responsibility.
- No restrain to accept responsibility.
- Accepting changes that helps the community as well as your institute.
- Consideration for others.
- Honesty in discharging proper ethical and social responsibility. George Washington once remarked that I hope I shall always possess firmness and virtue enough to maintain what I consider the most enviable of all titles, the character of an honest man.

- Equality among employees irrespective of their caste, creed, religion, gender, age etc.
- Cohesion among employees since they share common institutional vision and values.
- Democracy to express our opinions and views.
- Sovereignty to take decisions within the framework
- Concern for the upliftment and betterment of our society.
- Commitment towards work.

In short, values and principles are a holistic combination of veracity+ self will+ submissiveness and compassion.

## Decree 23: Maintain work life balance

> *"Balance is not better time management, but better boundary management. Balance means making choices and enjoying those choices."*
> *– Betsy Jacobson*

Always maintain a balance between your personal and professional life. Never let your personal problems affect your efficiency. Stay attentive and alert. Ensure that you don't bring your personal life to office. Commit yourself completely to your work when you are in the institute. Dr. Kathleen Hall once stated that we have overstretched our personal boundaries and forgotten that true happiness comes from living an authentic life fueled with a sense of purpose and balance.

Make certain that your stress is not affecting you physically or mentally, or your personal relationships with your family or friends. Identify various indicators of stress and find out various strategies to overcome it. Here are few simple steps to overcome your anxiety and stress.

- Identify the reason of your stress.
- Be determined to overcome it.
- Develop alternative solutions.
- Decide your deadline.
- Implement the best possible solution.

Identify those activities that help you to manage your stress like deep breathing, listening to music, talking to your friend etc. 10-20 minutes of physical exercise daily is highly recommended to overcome your stress. Share your problem (the most stressful one) with your senior; probably you may see some new elucidation to your troubles which can help you to overcome your fear and regain your positive spirit.

## Decree 24: Expect the unexpected

*"To expect the unexpected shows a thoroughly modern intellect."*
*– Oscar Wilde.*

Learn to expect *the* unexpected and don't be too surprised. Life isn't what it looks like at all times and things don't always turn out the way we suppose. Occasionally, the behaviour of our seniors may surprise us. When I say think positive, I don't mean that you anticipate only excellent things to ensue in your life. It means that in any circumstance, have a buoyant attitude to overcome the problem. Simultaneously, be prepared for disenchantment and no matter what happens, never get disheartened.

Also, learn the art of man management. Your seniors will appreciate it. The general traits of good teachers are the knowledge of teaching, empathy, keeping ego in check, communication skills, relationship skills, analytical skills, team spirit, ability to handle pressure and experience because often students are aggressive, impatient and they have a huge ego.

## Decree 25: Develop a you can attitude

*"Again, you can't connect the dots looking forward; you can only connect them looking backwards. So you have to trust that the dots will somehow connect in your future. You have to trust in something - your gut, destiny, life, karma, whatever. This approach has never let me down, and it has made all the difference in my life."*

*– Steve Jobs*

Many researchers have revealed that "external motivation" (like monetary or non monetary rewards) is not always a prime motivator for most of the employees. In fact "internally motivated" employees can do wonders for the institute. Thus, develop a positive attitude towards work. Believe in yourself. You are responsible for your own success or failure. We cannot direct the wind but we can adjust the sails. Put a stop on negative thinking.

Sometimes, it takes less time to fulfill the assigned task than finding an excuse for not performing the task or thinking too much about the results of non-performance. Avoid discontented people as much as possible as they spread negativity all around.

May be you stammered, felt nervous or conscious while giving a presentation, but appreciate yourself for trying and making a genuine effort. The same principle applies when others do the same mistakes. Accept their flaws as well. Try to find out what went wrong rather than who was wrong, fix the error and make sure you don't repeat such mistakes.

## Decree 26: Work with zeal and enthusiasm

*"A creative man is motivated by the desire to achieve, not by the desire to beat others"*
*– Ayn Rand.*

Don't hesitate to ask for help from your seniors, especially on difficult issues. Ask for their advice, views and valuable suggestions. Treat them as your mentors who can provide you practical feedback and the positives and negatives of your performance. Tell them that you would like to listen to your work evaluation, whether positive or negative. Occasionally ask your students whether or not they are happy with your teaching style. If not, let them suggest you some changes. Then, don't forget to thank them for their assistance in making your task simpler.

Be avid, organized and focused. Greet everyone with a smile. If you disagree with something, politely express your point of view. Buddha once believed that through zeal, knowledge is gotten; through lack of zeal, knowledge is lost.

Take initiatives. For example if there is any assignment that needs more help from people, volunteer yourself. Never try to get away from additional responsibilities. Challenge yourself every day. Look out for more duties and opportunities which is not a part of your current responsibility. Offer to help with any future events or assignments like annual day, Sports day, NCC, NACC visits etc. Volunteer your time to do something that's not a part of your work profile- your seniors will always appreciate it. Within the organization, enlarge your information system. Finally, don't brag about your past success. Put your knowledge in action which will benefit the institute.

An institute which doesn't have employees who possess A-Z qualities is likely to have a high employee turnover ratio. Satisfying your seniors takes substantial hard work, and if you want to win their faith, follow the above mentioned ways. Failure to follow any of these rules can abate your overall performance. Finally, a good teacher will set an example, adhere to proper code of conduct, accept ethical and social responsibility, work with authenticity, passion, proficiency, audacity and equanimity. All the best!

# 12 Ways to Effective Parent-Teacher Interaction

I dreamed I stood in a studio
And watched two sculptors there,
The clay they used was a young child's mind
And they fashioned it with care.

One was a teacher; the tools she used
were books and music and art;
One was a parent with a guiding hand
and a gentle loving heart.

And when at last their work was done
They were proud of what they had wrought
For the things they had worked into the child
Could never be sold or bought.

And each agreed she would have failed
if she had worked alone
For behind the parent stood the school,
and behind the teacher stood the home.

– Cleo V. Swarat

The two most significant forces in any child's life are parents and teachers. Researchers have revealed a positive impact of a partnership between teachers and parents resulting in better marks for students and helping them to overcome their problems. It also helps teachers in drafting better academic curriculum as they tend to understand their requirements properly. They also added that parents' involvement does have a direct impact on the child's intellectual accomplishments, wisdom, manners, actions and thoughts.

Teachers appreciate the efforts of parents who take interest in their child's development. Parents usually prefer meeting their child's teacher early in their school life but it should happen at all phases of their education. A teacher can very well nurture affiliations between parents, teachers, students and institute.

"No one has yet fully realized the wealth of sympathy, kindness, and generosity hidden in the soul of a child. The effort of every true education should be to unlock that treasure"- Emma Golmam.

I would like to suggest few strategies by which the institute can cultivate partnership between parents and teachers and break their communication barriers.

A. Welcome parents who come to interact with the teacher even without any formal invitation. Greet them and be glad about them for showing interest as active communication always boost parents involvement in their child's education. Remain enthusiastic, positive, open and supportive during meetings.

B. Teachers should never wait for parents-teachers meeting to be implicated in the institute. They can (with prior appointment) call the parents and can give valuable suggestions to augment their child's education.

"I am the child, all the world waits for my coming, all the earth watches with interest to see what I shall become.

*Civilization hangs in the balance, for what I am, the world of tomorrow will be".*

*- Mamie Gene Cole*

College teachers may think that students are mature enough to understand their accountability and duties and so their interaction with their parents is not necessary but the bad news is that though they are quite grown up, they rarely communicate with their parents about the college activities. Here teachers can play a proactive role to bridge the gap between the parents and their wards.

C. If personal visits are not possible, communicate via telephones, e-mails, sms and various other available technologies. Written communication is considered as the best way of interaction as it acts as a permanent reference (read written communication tips for further reference). Avoid using too many educational jargons as it might confuse them. The institute can send bulk sms or e-mail to the parents at least once in three months. The institute can also maintain an interactive voice response system or create an e-mail address to address parents' queries and to seek their feedback.

D. You should make certain that the institute continuously updates its website, shares all the valuable information, downloads the required information and ensures that there is a provision where they can add comments or feedback.

This gives an opportunity to parents who can't come to the institute regularly. Teachers can respond to them appropriately since sometimes due to communication barriers the teachers are often misunderstood by parents.

E. Parent-teacher meetings should not only be considered as reporting sessions but as a prospect to interact with parents regarding the student's strengths and weaknesses. John Ruskin once remarked that when love and skill work together, expect a masterpiece. A good parent-teacher rapport helps in developing mutual trust, support and a healthy relationship.

F. Teachers can request for feedback from parents on various areas like their child's growth, annual day/ sports day, celebration of grandparents day/ children's day or any other events conducted by the institute.

G. The teachers can introduce a bulletin and circular on behalf of the institute where they can share all the information about the forthcoming events. They can even add examination schedules. As someone rightly believed, it is not so much what is poured into the student, but what is planted that really counts.

H. Hyman Berston claimed teachers to be the child s third parent. So teacher's should not only communicate bad news like poor grades/ marks/ performance of the child but also commend their success and achievements which is a great form of encouragement not only for parents but also for students. While interacting with the parents, be careful about your remarks. Focus on the following.

- What the child was expected to achieve?
- What has he actually achieved?
- Are there any deviations?
- If yes, are they positive or negative?
- If the performance is more than expectations, appreciate his efforts.
- If less, find out the reason and suggest some ways by which the parents can help their child's learning.

If you are discussing any problem with parents, ask them for several ways to solve the problem and help the child as it is essential for the holistic development of the child. The parents come to know about the performance of their child in the institute through such interactions and the teachers know about the behaviour of their students in their homes from their parents.

I. Institutes should train their teacher's communication skills to interact with parents. During a conversation teachers must maintain proper body language; avoid using threatening words; try to evaluate the parent's perspective, be emphatic listener and try not to dishearten them.

J. In many developed countries like US, UK and Japan, a formal body comprising of parents and teachers is formed with a purpose to smoothen the progress of parental participation which is often referred as Parent-Teacher Association (PTA) or Parent- Teacher- Student Association (PTSA). Such programmes meetings, open-houses, conferences and get-togethers offer various opportunities for teachers and parents to share the problems of the children and mutually find some strategies to overcome them.

K. Such a structure can be adopted in our country too on a larger scale with an objective to:-

- Foster the all-round development of a child.
- Facilitate teaching and learning procedure.
- Create a mutual understanding between teachers and parents.
- Stimulate interest among parents.
- Make parents aware of their responsibilities at home for their child's development.
- Help parents to adapt themselves with the changing needs and the expectations of the child. As someone rightly said, drop a pebble in the water, just a splash and it is gone; But there's half-a-hundred ripples circling on and on and on, Spreading, spreading from the center, flowing on out to the sea. And there is no way of telling where the end is going to be.

L. Though a parent's participation has increased in the last few years. According to my research conducted on 75 parents. 35% parents did not interfere because they don't want to disturb the teachers and the students. 30% regretted that their feedback was never appreciated by teachers, whereas 15% of the parents remarked that they don't have enough time and the remaining said that they don't know how they can contribute in their child's development. When asked for their suggestions to overcome this problem as many as 70% of them said that it can be done by regularly attending the institutes' conferences/ meetings/ programs/ special days/ events etc. Whereas, the remaining believed that the institute should plan various activities, where parents can volunteer their time and participate. Few also stated that parents should be welcomed with humbleness and positivity.

I want to conclude that earier parent-teacher interactions were only limited to report card and quarterly/ half yearly meeting between the two but now they form an effective partnership to help the child succeed, get a good learning experience and demonstrate better understanding.

●●

# Myths and Realities

## Myth 1: Teaching is not a Profession

*Teaching creates all other professions.*
*– Anonymous*

**Reality:-** Wikipedia defines a professional as a person who is paid to undertake a specialized set of tasks and to complete them for a fee. The traditional professionals were doctors, lawyers, clergymen, and commissioned military officers. Today, the term is applied to estate agents, surveyors, environmental scientists, social workers, forensic scientists, educators, and many more.

A teacher is an individual who shares his/her knowledge and gives education to students. In many countries, teachers enjoy a status like other professionals. Teachers can be considered as professional's because of the following reasons.

- The role of a teacher is often official, recognised and enduring.
- In many countries, if you want to become a teacher, you need a professional degree/ certificate from a state or national university. This includes learning of human behaviour, and acquiring academic skills and competencies.
- They are often obligated to acquire specialized knowledge.
- They have to continuously update themselves and continue their education for personal development.
- They are required to follow certain ethical and moral codes of conduct.
- They require certain internal self motivation and self-esteem.
- Finally, they are experts in their specific area.

## Myth 2: I have to be perfect

*Who dares to teach must never cease to learn.*
– John Cotton Dana

**Reality:-** No doubt striving fof perfectionism can help you enhance your results and produce better output. However it is not possible to:-

- Never make any mistakes.

- Better than others.

This is because striving for perfectionism can sometimes lead to:-

- Low self confidence because we can never accept letdowns.
- Embarrassment or humiliation if we make any mistakes.
- Cynicism as we never want any discrepancies or variations in our lives.
- Gloominess because we always want to perform any task better than others.
- Stringency or firmness since we will perform only those tasks that we think we are perfect at.
- Compulsiveness in always being the best.
- Demotivation because we often fear failures and never accept new challenges.

According to me, our efforts should be limited to:-

- Always determining to be superlative.
- Achieving the best.
- Tolerating failures as a part of our lives.
- Committing ourselves to success.
- Accepting ourself as we are.
- Forgiving our mistakes.
- Accommodating failures and learning from them.
- Building our confidence and patience.
- Acknowledging the fact that human beings are full of limitations, divergences, weaknesses, flaws and inaccuracies.
- Focusing on the bigger picture and overlooking minor mistakes.
- Remembering Pareto's 80:20 principle that 80% of the task takes 20% of your time and efforts, whereas the remaining 20% task drains 80% exertion.

## Myth 3: I should know all the answers

*"We don't know all the answers. If we knew all the answers we'd be bored, wouldn't we? We keep looking, searching, trying to get more knowledge."*
*– Jack LaLanne*

**Reality:-** It's true you are expected to know everything. As a teacher, it is your duty to enlarge the scope of student's understanding and knowledge. You can tutor them to take responsibility for their manners, conduct, performance, thoughts as well as crudities. Knowledge is the real power. In this age, you may not know all the answers to student queries. If someone raises some question to which you don't know the answer, never overreact or prove student's question to be irrelevant or pass any false information. Calm down.

According to me, if you don't know something, accepting it and trying to find the answer is the real power. Get ready for some homework. Return with an answer in your next class. It will also pass a positive signal that you consider student questions important and want to answer them.

For any particular query, you can even involve your students to work together and find the answer. This will give them an opportunity to be involved in the learning process, and probably if they can't bring a comprehensive answer, they will at least contribute something relevant related to the topic.

Whether you are a fresher or an experienced teacher, admitting that you don't know the answer is never reprehensible. Allow your students to ask questions and keep trying to learn something new to explore your potential to the fullest.

## Myth 4: I can always change the students

*"Consider how hard it is to change yourself and you'll understand what little chance you have of trying to change others."*
*– Jacob Braude*

**Reality:-**You want to change others for their good. Many of us wish that demotivated pessimists should change. This will make our lives much simpler and will definitely benefit them in long run. Some teachers spend their valuable time and efforts to change others' thoughts and behaviour, but most of the time, it's disappointing and frustrating, and you eventually end up being annoyed and displeased.

You are depending on their attitude and behaviour for being happy and if things don't happen your way, you will blame them for your failures. Also, changing others will not assure constructive outcome.

Most of the times, you can transform others by altering your personal conduct. An ideal situation is to take responsibility of most circumstances yourself.

Practice before you preach. Bring to an end your unproductive activities by accepting accountability for your personal failure. One of the best ways to solve the problem is to collectively design an action plan and ensure that you implement them. However, this doesn't mean you have to sacrifice your ideas for understanding and accommodating others.

## Myth 5: I have to always be good to others

*A teacher affects eternity; he can never tell where his influence stops.*
*– Henry Brooks Adams*

**Reality:-** Understand what "good" really is, what it stands for to you and what it takes to be really good. It can be based on your own ethical and moral ideals. It can sometimes contradict with other's beliefs and opinions. What you think is right can be wrong for others (some may consider that lying to save others is right). Always support what is right, fair and true. Don't just do something because your seniors say its right; or because your recognition is at stake or because you want to be "good".

You will get immense contentment if you support the right over wrong, fair over unfair, ethical over unethical and good over bad. Just remember that you have to be "fair, true, ethical and right" and not just "good". If you are not doing bad things, it doesn't mean you are a very good human being. To be a good individual, you also have to stop someone from doing the same. It can be hurtful in the beginning, but will definitely yield positive results in the long run. So sometimes, you have to be "strict" rather than good.

For instance:- if you find some student cheating in an examination, you may think of forgiving him/her because if you complain, he/she might be debarred or expelled from the institute. But, they will never learn any lesson in their lives and continue the same in all the exams. So, do consider the long term impact of your decision on that particular student and on other students.

## Myth 6: I have to be right all the time

*In teaching, you cannot see the fruit of a day's work.*
*It is invisible and remains so, maybe for twenty years.*
*– Jacques Barzun*

**Reality:-** One section of the people in this world think they are always right. Are you one of them? Is your "always being right" attitude annoying others and sometimes yourself. Choose your response shrewdly. If yes... the good news is that you can always change it. It's difficult to be always right. Never develop a dogmatic attitude and draw pleasure by proving others wrong. This can easily ruin your relationship with others. At times, it becomes a tool of defending yourself, in which case, it becomes even worse.

**For example:-** if you are unable to finish your syllabus on time, you blame the institute, colleagues, seniors students and even the university for personal failure, which are illogical several times. You don't accept being wrong and blame others for it. The real question is, "did you draft and implement your session plan properly to meet your deadlines". So here are few ways in which you can change your attitude.

- Be a good listener. When someone is discussing something, never dismiss his/her ideas completely or get into any debate. It can sometimes be a short lived triumph with no applause or appreciation.
- If you think you are right, but somewhere you are not happy with your action, words, choice, or decision, that's probably because you were wrong. So listen to your consciousness.
- Don't think you have to be right even if your mind says you are wrong. True success comes not by proving others wrong and yourself right.
- Sportingly admit if you were wrong. If you don't admit being wrong, you will repeat the same mistake again.
- Accept the fact that you will fail sometimes and take responsibility for it.

## Myth 7: Only students have to listen

*The mediocre teacher tells. The good teacher explains.*
*The superior teacher demonstrates. The great teacher inspires.*
*– William Arthur Ward*

**Reality:-** It is an old belief that students have to quietly listen to the knowledge of the teacher and teachers are the ones who speak. Teaching is not just transferring of facts and figures from educator to students. How well you hear, comprehend and evaluate student contribution has a direct impact on your efficiency. With better listening you can easily:-

- Persuade and encourage your students,
- Reduce misapprehensions,
- Easily identify student expectations
- Identify whether you are meeting their expectation or not.
- Build better rapport with them.
- Clear their doubts, answer their queries, and resolve any problems they have encountered in class.

Never interrupt the speaker, be it your student, colleagues or seniors. When we listen to others, we promote their self-confidence by cheering a helpful and effectual communication. Stay active by answering questions of the speaker and maintain eye contact.

Treat each student with admiration and compassion, as they have their personal identity. If someone raises a question in the class, or shares some information related to the topic, support them to carry on communication (through your body language) to demonstrate that you are interested and listening. It will also boost the confidence of the speaker. If you like the students' point, give prompt feedback by appreciating his query or for sharing some meaningful information.

## Myth 8: I am always motivated

*The first duty of a university is to teach wisdom,*
*no trade; character, not technicalities."*
*– Winston Churchill.*

**Reality:-** We all need constant motivation to accomplish our objective. It's like a fuel in your vehicle. You have to fill the fuel regularly. Similarly you have to constantly motivate yourself. Certainly you need intelligence, academic and general knowledge to be a good teacher. But, if you lack motivation, everything is vain. Motivation can be internal and external.

External motivation is mainly dependent on monetary factors like award, money or incentives whereas; internal motivation develops an ability to push yourself to overcome all the challenges in life. It provides emotional and physical strength one needs to overcome all the obstacles. The more internally motivated you are, the more passion you have to reach your goals. External motivation is temporary in nature and is short lived. Researchers have revealed that any internally motivated individual performs better than the externally motivated ones. So here are few ways to constantly motivate yourself.

- Find out your personal motivational tool that is uncomplicated and swift. The aspiration to mentor their students by positively influencing them and being their role model is a longing of many teachers.
- Derive pleasure from your work. Never lose your enthusiasm.
- Enjoy yourself and find pleasure in your work. If you don't like your profession, how can you expect others to like you or your vocation?
- Observe your seniors, colleagues or read inspiring stories of successful people and learn few lessons from them.
- Don't regularly use fear as a motivational technique.
- Get out of your comfort zone and grasp every opportunity to learn something new and enrich your skills.
- Be kind and gentle to others.
- Decide your short term and long term goals.
- Learn to accept challenges.

Always try to be internally motivated. It is easier to stay motivated since you are determined by your own values and goals.

## Myth 9: I don't have to prepare

*Don't try to fix the students, fix ourselves first. The good teacher makes the poor student good and the good student superior. When our students fail, we, as teachers, too, have failed.*

*– Marva Collins*

**Reality:-** Researchers have revealed direct affirmative correlation between teachers' knowledge in their subject and their performance in the classroom. Whether you are a fresher or an experienced teacher, the best way to build your confidence and retain it is to be prepared for each class. Preparation will also help to reduce your stress.

Some chapters need to be taught without simply following the textbooks as you might want your students to learn and apply their learning in real world and not just memorize few facts and figures to clear their exams. You have to convert a difficult or boring topic into appealing and acceptable for which you must have a daily/weekly/monthly plan with certain degree of flexibility. Before each lecture, ask yourself the following questions.

- How much academic and general knowledge you should have?
- Should certain topics be more focused than others?

- Do I need any additional preparation for a particular subject or topic? If yes, how should I prepare myself?

You can generate interest for the subject by explaining them the benefits, its practical application and occasionally adopting different coaching techniques. Don't forget to carry a bag of patience along with your books. Have the fortitude and compliance to dedicate additional time and hard work essential for triumph of the students and institute.

## Myth 10: I don't have to be IT savvy

*Helpdesk:* Double click on "My Computer"

*User:* I can't see your computer.

*Helpdesk:* No, double click on "My Computer" on your computer.

*User:* Huh?

*Helpdesk:* There is an icon on your computer labeled "My Computer". Double click on it.

*User:* What's your computer doing on mine?

**Reality:-** Many institutes are increasing their expenditures on information technology because they have realized the fact that with the use of information technology, their productivity and efficiency will increase. So now, they prefer to recruit staffs that have at least basic computer knowledge. You are teaching a computer savvy generation and hence you should have basic computer know-how not only to meet their expectations, but also to relate to them. Few benefits of using IT for your session are:-

- It can easily engage students.
- It can increase students' participation and enthusiasm.
- It can be a creative form of learning and teaching.
- It helps the teachers in their research projects.
- It demonstrates that the teacher is willing to try new things for the betterment of students.

However, technology is just an aid to your teaching. It can't completely replace good teaching. Technology should be used to augment the teacher's competence and efficacy. A sensible teacher will clearly decide what technology she/he wants to use and avoid. According to me, you must possess some general technology knowledge and skills like:-

i. Use of PowerPoint presentation to aid your oral and written communication

ii. Use of e-mail to send, receive and enclose documents.

iii. Use of Internet to download desired information.

iv. Use of Internet based word processing programs.

v. Use of basic functions like cut, copy, paste, printing selected documents, creating folder retrieving files, use of spell check, deleting documents, use of caps lock and use of thesaurus.

vi. Use of spread sheets for mathematic operations and for creating charts, diagrams, graphs etc.

## Myth 11: Anyone can be a good teacher

*I like a teacher who gives you something to take home to think about besides homework.*
*– Lily Tomlin as "Edith Ann"*

**Reality:-** Good teachers make a big difference in a student's learning and development. They prepare their students to "think global and act local". Their aspiration is to prepare their students to confront and meet the requirements in a modern workplace. They teach their students effective communication, team work, mutual cooperation, analytical and problem solving techniques. I analyzed the characteristics of a good teacher as the following.

| | |
|---|---|
| great friend | tolerant |
| optimistic | enthusiasm |
| open minded | affirmative |
| cheerful and creative | helpful and humble |
| disciplined | efficient |

A good teacher is mature enough to handle few impatient students. They never take anything personally, especially the behaviour or attitude of nasty students. If students don't understand something, they have the patience to repeat it again and again.

A teacher should never tolerate childishness or disorderliness of any student, however, they need marvelous endurance with genuine students who are really finding the content difficult to understand. They never allow students to slag-off or bad-mouth other teachers. They never say, "It's not my job" because they prepare students not only for exams, but also for life. They want their students to be good human beings and not just memorizers of theory.

## Myth 12: Subject knowledge is sufficient

*Teachers are expected to reach unattainable goals with inadequate tools. The miracle is that at times, they accomplish this impossible task.*

*- Haim G. Ginott*

**Reality:**-Your subject knowledge is vital because you can't teach what you don't know. You have to continuously build an understanding of your subject and related areas because your students can easily assess all the information on their phones or computers using Internet. They need to associate their learning to everyday life.

In-depth subject knowledge includes knowing the theories, application of theories, principles and concepts of your subject.

Teachers who possess good knowledge related to their subject can go beyond textbooks, involve students in meaningful discussions and can make the class interactive. Your responsibility as a teacher is not only to share subject knowledge and few facts and figures, but strive for true education, which essentially requires you.

- To create a desired learning experience for students
- To build a strong foundation for students so that their ethical and moral standards are high.
- To make students responsible citizens of the nation who contribute to the betterment of the society.
- To teach students to respect others, especially elders.
- To give students an opportunity to identify and search for new information.
- To broaden their horizon.
- To prepare them to take decisions rationally through vital elucidation and analysis.

## Myth 13: All teachers are the same

*The dream begins with a teacher who believes in you,*
*who tugs and pushes and leads you to the next plateau,*
*sometimes poking you with a sharp stick called "truth."*
*– Dan Rather*

**Reality:-** All teachers are never the same. Students may encounter emotional, moral, social, mental and physical ups and downs through the growing years. Only a decent teacher can accept these changes among students and respond to them aptly. The achievement of higher education depends on the knowledge of previous education. Hence, right from the inception years, they set a right foundation for every child. They offer blueprint to students to help them achieve success by assisting them to set better goals for their future and also help them in creating an action plan to achieve their targets. They take pride in student s accomplishment and believe in a holistic development of each student. The following are the qualities of a good teacher.

1. intelligence
2. patience
3. wisdom
4. enthusiasm
5. time management
6. team player
7. Open to change

8. creativity and innovativeness
9. flexibility
10. self confidence
11. communication skills
12. high ethical and moral values
13. planning and implementation skills
14. leadership
15. negotiation skills
16. stress management skills
17. good sense of humor
18. positive attitude
19. stability
20. evenhandedness
21. integrity
21. classroom management
22. determination
23. selflessness
24. commitment and dedication
25. listening skills
26. being organized
27. hard worker
28. encouraging and motivating others
29. willingness to learn, unlearn and relearn
30. reverential.
31. technology savvy
32. friend, philosopher and guide
33. maturity
34. punctuality
35. accepting moral and social responsibility
36. willingness to help others
37. integrating practical and theoretical knowledge
38. specialized subject knowledge
39. professional approach

## Myth 14: Teaching is easier as compared to other profession

*If a doctor, lawyer, or dentist had 40 people in his office at one time, all of whom had different needs, and some who didn't want to be there and were causing trouble, and the doctor, lawyer, or dentist, without assistance, had to treat them all with professional excellence for nine months, then he might have some conception of the classroom teacher's job.*

*-Donald D. Quinn*

**Reality:-** The Oxford English Dictionary defines a profession as "a paid occupation, especially one that involves prolonged training and a formal qualification". Let's compare the desirable traits, aspects and distinctiveness necessary for the success of professionals like doctors, CAs, engineers with teachers:-

| | Qualities | Other Professions | Teachers |
|---|---|---|---|
| **Professional attributes** | | | |
| 1. | Expertise in particular area | ✓ | ✓ |
| 2. | Specialized knowledge | ✓ | ✓ |
| 3. | Formal education | ✓ | ✓ |
| 4. | Theoretical and practical skills | ✓ | ✓ |
| 5. | Knowledge about their industry | ✓ | ✓ |
| 6. | High quality work (efficiency) | ✓ | ✓ |
| 7. | Professional ethics | ✓ | ✓ |
| 8. | Work morale and motivation | ✓ | ✓ |
| 9. | Permanent career | ✓ | ✓ |
| 10. | Intelligence and wisdom | ✓ | ✓ |
| **Personal attributes** | | | |
| 1. | Positive attitude | ✓ | ✓ |
| 2. | Personal interest and desire | ✓ | ✓ |
| 3. | Patience | ✓ | ✓ |
| 4. | Responsiveness | ✓ | ✓ |
| 5. | Accountability | ✓ | ✓ |
| 6. | Enthusiasm | ✓ | ✓ |
| 7. | Time management skills | ✓ | ✓ |
| 8. | Team player | ✓ | ✓ |
| 9. | Accepting challenges | ✓ | ✓ |
| 10. | Accommodating changes | ✓ | ✓ |

| | | | |
|---|---|---|---|
| 11. | Listening skills | ✓ | ✓ |
| 12. | Trustworthiness | ✓ | ✓ |
| 13. | Integrity | ✓ | ✓ |
| 14. | Dependability | ✓ | ✓ |
| 15. | Maturity | ✓ | ✓ |
| 16. | Analytical and thinking skills | ✓ | ✓ |
| 17. | Philanthropic approach | ✓ | ✓ |

From the above table, it can be concluded that teaching requires all the professional and personal characteristics that are needed in other professions. Hence, teaching is not easier than any other profession.

## Myth 15: I should never make any mistake

*To teach is to learn twice.*
*– Joseph Joubert*

**Reality:-** Some people always strive for perfection and are scared of making even the smallest error. Are you one of them? If yes, then I must say by trying to avoid mistakes, you are actually restricting yourself to try and avoid new things. Frankly, there are two approaches to look at any mistake - an optimistic way and a pessimist way. For an optimist, a mistake is a learning experience, but for a pessimist, it can be a reason to be criticized. After any mistake, they feel awful, annoyed or aggravated. Here are few techniques by which you can master the art of making mistakes and learning from them.

- Accept the fact that mistakes are not horrific or something to be evaded.
- After every mistake, feel thrilled because you have got an opportunity to learn something new.
- Just work hard to ensure that you don't repeat the same mistake again.
- Have the audacity to try something new, but be alert of the depressing result of your actions. Guts also signify accepting responsibilities for personal failures.
- Trust yourself even after breakdowns. If you don't believe in yourself, you will lose the enthusiasm of finding different ways to do new things.
- Never be culpable, apologetic or depressed for any mistake because it can waste your valuable time and energy.
- Learn to split inaccuracies from opportunities and you will have mastered the skill of learning from mistakes.
- Never give up. Keep the bigger picture in mind and don't be defeated by temporary letdowns. Just because of one mistake, don't lose the pleasure of chasing your dreams and accomplishing your aspirations.

●●

# Articles on Teachers

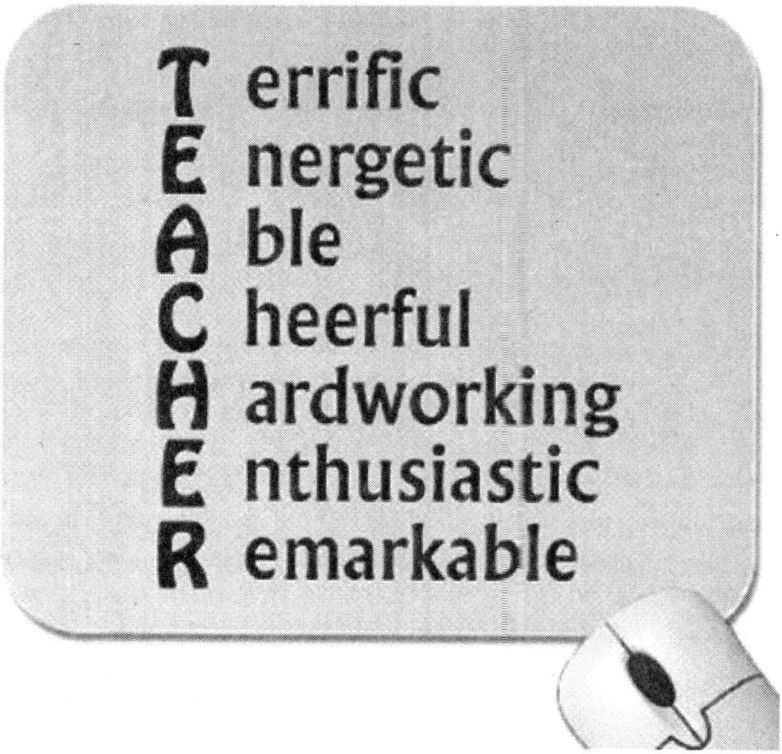

**T** errific
**E** nergetic
**A** ble
**C** heerful
**H** ardworking
**E** nthusiastic
**R** emarkable

## Article 1:Be a pro-change teacher

*Professor Joe Martin*

Many teachers (especially experienced ones) suffer from what I call "change phobia." And if not carefully monitored, even new teachers can be inflicted with this the career-ending disease. What is "change phobia" you ask? It's exactly what you may think it is; it's an unhealthy fear of change. As teachers, we can't afford to be "change phobics"; the nature of our job dictates that we must remain open to change (sometimes at a moment's notice). But what if you're not used to it or don't know where to start? Well, I'm glad you asked, because here's something I want you to try.

I want to you to do an exercise with your class I call "Teacher for a day." The effectiveness of this exercise depends on the maturity level of your class (and your receptiveness). I would think 4th grade and above would work fine, but I'll let you make the call.

Have your students take out a blank sheet of paper, and then I want you to write this question on the board: "If I was the teacher for a day... this is what I would do to make our class more fun and educational?"

Have each student write down at least one to three ideas on their sheet of paper and turn it in with their names on it. It doesn't have to be written in narrative form; it could be written as a list of items, as long as it's legible. This shouldn't take more than 10 minutes. After they turn in their papers, take them home with you, and see what ideas make the most sense and are the most realistic to implement. Then simply determine how you can (and will) incorporate those ideas (i.e., changes) into your lesson plan.

I must warn you to prepare yourself to be shocked by the creative (even weird) ideas you're going to receive from your students. Also, as an added (and optional) bonus, announce which students came up with the best and most creative ideas, and give them some special gift, treat, or prize. Trust me, after you implement a few of these ideas, I guarantee you'll reduce the chances of ever becoming (or return to being) a "change phobic."

## Article 2: Simple but effective ways to be a great teacher

Looking to really connect with your students?

1) **A great teacher will always be there-** If you are not in your classroom, you are not teaching. Yes, teachers must take days off occasionally, but do not make it a habit. If you are feeling a little sick, unless it is serious, show up! A sick regular teacher is ten times better for his or her students than a healthy substitute. Regular attendance is a must. Be proud to have a perfect attendance record.

2) **A great teacher is accessible-** You need to help your students at all times. That means before school, during lunch, and after school. No, you do not have to do it all the time. Start out with something like two days a week before school, lunch, and after school. You are the best tutor your students can get. Teach them.

3) **Great teachers know their students on a personal basis-** Talk to them during lessons. What is their favorite music? TV? Movies? Talk to them in the hallways. The more you know, the more you can adapt. It is easy to converse during class time. Little comments between concepts can go a long way. If some show up early for class, you can really get personal. No class time? Pass out a questionnaire. Above all, learn their names quickly.

4) **A great teacher knows many parents**- Get phone numbers. Make two calls a day to parents. If you can, make more. They do not need to be long. Just a short hello and that you are interested in their child. In just a short time, you can indeed make contact to at least one parent of each student. Parents can be your biggest allies. Students will perform and behave better if they know you are talking to their parents.

5) **A great teacher knows what they are teaching-** If you do not know what you are doing, how can you teach? This involves complete preparation.

6) **A Great Teacher Attends School Events**- Make yourself seen at school sports and performances. Being seen in this setting shows students you care about them and support them.

7) **A great teacher lives in or visits the neighborhood**- If you do not live in the same place as your school, make some visits on weekends. Go to a local place to eat. Shop at a local store. Many of your students may have parents who own local businesses. Patronize them. Visit a church. The more your students see you, the more they will be willing to behave in class. They will see you as someone who is willing to come down to their level.

8) **A great teacher eats lunch on campus**- Wander around at lunch and sit at a student table. Buy a school lunch and join them. Many students help sell food. Make a point to buy something.

9) **A great teacher is always fair**- Expect the best, but be flexible. Fairness does not have to mean leniency. It simply means to grade your students on a balanced scale.

10) **Great teachers never lose their cool**- Bite your tongue. All things will pass. Never carry a grudge. Things in your classroom will happen. This goes hand in hand with being a professional. Acting like a raving lunatic is a sure way to shorten your career.

## Article 3: Teach it forward and reap it forever

*Professor Joe Martin*

Sometimes the smallest gifts are the greatest gifts. I should know, because my physical education teacher made an impact on my life that I have not yet forgotten. I had just completed my final exam (don't ask me why we had to take a written exam in P.E.). When I attempted to turn to my teacher Coach Bruce passed a hand-written note to me.

He insisted that I do not open it and asked me to read it later. Bewildered, I just agreed and proceeded to leave. Later that afternoon, as I stood in my room getting ready to change into something more comfortable, I felt the note Coach Bruce had given me stuffed in my back pocket. I immediately proceeded to read it. The note said the following: "Joe, it was an absolute pleasure to have you in my class this year. Your attitude and work ethic was a joy to watch. I can't tell you how much I looked forward to seeing you everyday.

The reason I wrote you this note is because I'm not sure if I'll ever get a chance to speak to you again. However, I just want you to know that I am certain I will be reading about you and seeing your face again, because I know you're going to do some extraordinary things in your life and impact a lot of people. So when you do become 'famous" you'll know that I was first to say 'I told you so.' Good luck and God bless." My initial reaction was the same as yours, "Wow." Then my reaction moved from disbelief to pride. For the first time, in a long time, I felt there was greatness in me. As a child, I suffered from low self-esteem, and I wanted desperately to win the approval of others, especially men; because my father wasn't an active parent.

I can't tell you what Coach Bruce's letter did for my spirit, my self-esteem, and my attitude towards school. Yeah, it was just P.E., but for some reason it represented much more than that. I saved his note and carried it with me throughout college, eventually graduating at the top of my class and being voted "Most Outstanding Student" in my major.

As a result of Coach Bruce's impact, when I became a teacher, I quickly made it a tradition to pick one student in each of my classes (not necessarily the one with the highest grade), and give him or her a similar note on the last day of class. All I can say now is I know how Coach Bruce must have felt when he gave the note to me. I seem to get as much pleasure out of giving it to my students as I did receiving it from Coach Bruce.

As a new teacher (or even a veteran one), I encourage you today to look for unique ways to encourage a student, colleague, or administrator at your school. I guarantee you. You'll be making a down payment on a future blessing.

## Article 4: A great teacher essay

Throughout my life I have been taught by a number of teachers, all of whom have had some form of influence on me whether it be positive or negative. However, through this intellectual journey I have discovered many qualities that have distinguished these great teachers from the rest.

A great teacher has certain qualities that distinguish him/her from the other teachers. He/she shows qualities such as patience, kindness, flexibility, resourcefulness, tolerance and open-mindedness. He/she also has a good sense of humour and is honest, humble, enthusiastic and most importantly enjoys teaching. A great teacher always smiles at his/her pupils and dedicates him/herself to the job.

One special quality that I have most often found in a great teacher is that they are able to be my friend. I do not know anyone better to trust and gain knowledge from than a friend. A friend is often a person that you remember for the rest of your life. However, I also believe that there must remain a balance between representing an authority and being a friend, so that the student shows respect. Some of the best teachers that I have been taught by, have shown motherly or fatherly love towards their students. This attribute, in particular, is something that makes a really great teacher. One of my most memorable teachers was from grade five, named

Mrs. Chinnevai. At one point during that year I remember having a very difficult time dealing with the death of my grandpa and she was able to comfort me and talk to me at a time when I needed it most. Whenever I just needed to talk to her, she made herself available and that made me feel like she really cared about me and that my feelings mattered to her.

For me, a good teacher is someone who teaches not only with their mind but also with their heart. This is a person who truly cares about his/her pupils and their interests, wishes and feelings and is also someone that a student can confide in times of sadness or of joy. It is great for a teacher to be able to get to know each one of his/her students personally in order to help them with their problems.

## Article 5: Teach outside your comfort zone

*Professor Joe Martin*

It was the middle of school year, and I was going through a rough stretch when it seemed like nothing I tried was working with one particular class I taught. I must note that although I wasn't a beginner, I was still considered a new teacher with less than three years of experience. I found myself complaining to a colleague who always seemed to possess a positive attitude no matter what the circumstances. I told him that I felt very uncomfortable about the progress of my class, and many of them seemed to be lacking the necessary basic skills to master the subject.

He proceeded to share a simple philosophy that has transformed, not only my teaching career, but my personal life as well. He suggested that having a challenging class like the one I had was more of a blessing than a burden. He asked me, "Has this class made you more or less creative?" Of course, I said, "more." He asked, "Has this class caused you to be more or less resourceful?" Again, I replied, "more." He continued, "Has this class led you to pray more or less?" And of course, I laughed and said, "more." And then he made his point.

He told me that the last thing a new teacher ever wants to become is "comfortable." He said that "comfort" breeds complacency, which leads to a false sense of security. He said that whenever we get comfortable, we tend to develop a false sense of confidence (i.e., security), believing we're in full control of a situation. Often, this false sense of security allow us to take things for granted, including our class.

He wasn't saying this was the case always, but I agree that if we take a closer look at it, as it relates to a marriage, it makes perfect sense. When couples first start dating, each person usually works hard to figure out what the other person likes or dislikes, and looks for creative and thoughtful ways to please the other person – no matter how difficult it may be. But what happens when we "figure out" the other person? We often stop doing the very thing(s) that won their heart in the first place.

I believe teaching can be viewed the same way. Often, when a subject, lesson, or class becomes so easy, it's easy to shift into a pattern of "cruise control." We've all known that one veteran teacher who hasn't changed his or her curriculum, handouts, films, and/or tests in 15+ years. This type of attitude of complacency can sometimes lead us not to push ourselves to a higher level of excellence.

The truth is, when everything's comfortable, we actually believe we're in control of things. But when things get uncomfortable, God gently reminds us of who's really in control. Comfort is good, but remember, it's not the goal. The goal is constant and never-ending improvement. Such a simple shift in our thinking can make a huge difference in our performance both in and outside of the classroom. So step outside your "comfortable teaching box" and thank God for the "tough ones".

## Article 6: Quality of teaching is at the core of school improvement. Dave Weston discusses how schools can get it right and what Ofsted are looking for:

'Great teaching is easy to recognize, but hard to define. The truth is that there are as many great teaching styles as there are great teachers. The effort to find a one-size-fits-all recipe for classroom success is therefore fruitless' (John C Jeffries, Virginia Law School, 1973).

Every primary school and head teacher hopes that teaching in their school is outstanding and aspires for an 'outstanding' judgment from Ofsted. A key factor in achieving outstanding status is the quality of teaching and learning. The Ofsted grade descriptors for outstanding teaching include a focus on pupils making exceptional progress as a result of inspiring teaching, from teachers having excellent subject knowledge and the innovative use of new technology.

Outstanding teaching looks different depending on the circumstances and context. An outstanding KS2 maths lesson on algebra will look very different to an outstanding KS1 PE lesson. However, outstanding teaching and learning underpins every effective school. Research shows that all the best teachers motivate their pupils to work hard and assess them regularly. How teachers use pupil assessments to plan and shape future lessons is an important factor in outstanding teaching. This is one aspect of the culture of outstanding schools.

Whole-school factors contributing to outstanding teaching

Highly effective teaching is usually only consistently seen in schools where there is positive and thoughtful leadership. Two years ago Ofsted identified the characteristics of very effective primary schools in challenging circumstances and these features included the following factors:

- A structured environment which provides stability and purpose.
- An environment which develops self-belief and confidence.

  Teaching pupils the things they really need to know (by taking charge of the curriculum) and showing them how to learn for themselves.
- A place which gives opportunities, responsibilities and develops trust (for both pupils and staff).

  A place which listens to pupils and acts on what they say.

  An organisation which builds bridges with parents, families and communities, working in partnership with other professionals.

- An organisation which has high aspirations, expectations and achievement and has a positive 'can-do' culture, where praise and encouragement prevail and self-esteem is high.
- Ofsted also stressed the crucial role of the quality of leadership: 'There is no denying the pivotal role of the headteacher in creating the ethos of the school and in exercising strong pedagogical leadership' (Twenty Successful Primary Schools in Challenging Circumstances, Ofsted, 2009).
- The key features of outstanding teachers

  The TES carried out some research in 2009 looking at the key features of highly effective teachers. The research, headed 'The Seven Secrets of Great Teaching', was similar to the approach of Steven Covey in his book The Seven Habits of Highly Effective People. It showed that very good teachers could deliver outstanding lessons due to the use of a variety of key skills. These included:
- Building confidence

  Effective teachers are very good at building pupils self-esteem. For one head teacher in the research, building confidence (for both pupils and staff) was part of her personal and professional ethos. This was based on celebrating success and achievement.
- Ability to make difficult decisions

  The outstanding teachers exhibited the strength of being able to make difficult or unpopular decisions.
- Developing others

  This behaviour is collectively the most prominent among teachers. It's about developing your own and others' capabilities by providing opportunities, and this was the area that successful teachers were most confident of doing. An example of this is when teachers give up their own time to help other colleagues acquire new skills or deal with difficult pupils. An interesting quote from one of the teachers involved in the research was, 'Everyone's got their own strengths and in the schools that I've worked in; we always make the most of them by supporting colleagues'.
- Good communicators

  The key skill of good communication was identified as a significant factor in effective teaching. Many successful teachers gave examples of using songs, analogies and multi-media displays to communicate with and engage pupils. One head had effectively used the song 'Proud' by Heather Small to convey a message of confidence throughout the school.
- Being nonconformists

  A large number of successful teachers were classified by the research as nonconformists, as they enjoyed trying out new ideas. This quality goes against the norm, as teachers are often faced with perceived timetabling restrictions and curriculum boundaries. The role of school leadership was considered vital in the creation of an environment where innovation is valued and encouraged to allow excellent teachers to succeed.

- They thrive in the company of others

  Good teachers enjoy the company of others, both teachers and pupils, and often have some extrovert personality traits. This links in well with being a good communicator and indicates 'fellowship' towards others and that most teachers thrive on working with colleagues.

- They see the 'bigger picture'

  Interestingly enough, the selected teachers in the project were strong at looking at the bigger picture, rather than the minute details of planning or administration. They were keen to see good practice in others' schools and counties and were always proactive rather than reactive.

**Indicators of outstanding teaching**

In Ofsted terms an outstanding lesson is one with many significant strengths and no areas for improvement. This should also be very closely linked with clear evidence of effective learning and progress for every learner in the class. It is often more important to focus on what the pupils are doing than what the teacher is doing. What the pupils do and learn in a lesson is often a better indicator of the quality of a lesson. The key factors include:

- Are the pupils highly engaged?
- Do they move from listening to being positively motivated?
- Do they learn and make progress?
- Do they obviously enjoy the lesson and have fun, and are they keen to discuss what they have learned and what they might be doing in the next lesson?
- Do the pupils ask appropriate (and challenging) questions?
- Do they show a keen interest in the tasks?
- Are they proud of their work?
- Are the pupils involved in deciding any part/content of the next lesson on the topic?

Effective teachers who obtain an outstanding grade from inspectors add value to lessons by using special approaches and features. These are usually on top of the normal good teaching approaches and may include some of the following:

- subject expertise and flair
- the involvement of every pupil in the learning process
- intelligent questioning involving every pupil
- the use of a wide variety of resources as appropriate including new technology
- involving pupils in the learning process and developing independent learning.

## What makes an outstanding lesson?

Ask an average class teacher and they might say, 'A lesson which is well planned, has the buzz factor and in which the pupils behave well.' Ask a pupil and they might say, 'A lesson which is fun and in which we learn something.' Ask some head teachers and you may receive the answer, 'A lesson which carefully follows the school teaching and learning policy and fulfils all the Ofsted grade criteria.' Ask an inspector, and you might hear, 'the teacher displays outstanding subject knowledge and challenges and enthuses pupils, and assessment indicates that the whole class have made significant progress.'

This shows how difficult it is to succinctly define the outstanding lesson, but many of these features are found in very effective teaching.

An interesting model on what contributes towards an outstanding lesson can be based on Maslow's hierarchy of needs. An outstanding lesson can be described as a lesson where appropriate resources are used by a teacher who is enthusiastic about their subject in delivering a learning experience which takes into account the varying needs of each pupil and inspires them to take risks, make connections and learn while constantly checking that they are meeting high expectations and are becoming independent learners.

Relating this to Maslow's hierarchy would indicate that the base of the pyramid would include appropriate resources and subject knowledge and enthusiasm. The next layer would include planning and differentiation to ensure personalized learning. The next would relate to communication and motivation and would emphasize learners evaluating their own progress. The apex of the pyramid would include high aspiration and expectation with the overall aim of developing independent and reflective learning. This indicates the varying skills that the highly effective teacher needs to demonstrate to deliver outstanding lessons.

## Outstanding teaching in the 2009 Ofsted framework

The 2009 Ofsted framework for inspection expects inspectors to evaluate how well teaching promotes learning, progress and enjoyment for all pupils. They are expected to look carefully at the range of teaching styles and activities and to what extent they sustain pupils' concentration, motivation and application. Ofsted state that judgments about the quality of teaching cannot be made in isolation.

The quality of teaching is linked closely to the context, including behaviour, assessment and, crucially, school leadership and management. There is an emphasis that when evaluating teaching, inspectors should focus on the impact on pupils' learning. A key question asked by Ofsted which is very relevant is: 'What are different groups and individual pupils actually learning as opposed to doing?' (Guidance to Inspectors, Ofsted, 2009)

For outstanding teaching Ofsted expects pupils to understand in detail how to improve their work and that they are consistently supported in doing so. The role of the teacher should have a striking impact on the quality of learning of pupils.

## Outstanding teaching in the proposed 2012 Ofsted framework

The draft proposals for the new Ofsted framework (due to be implemented in January 2012) talk about strong leadership creating the climate in which effective teaching and pupil achievement flourish. It also refers to the need for effective leaders knowing their school well and having high expectations and setting ambitious targets for raising standards.

Leaders will be expected to monitor teaching and learning rigorously and track pupils' progress meticulously. There seems to be more emphasis on monitoring and tracking rather than teaching styles.

There is an increased expectation that effective leadership will focus on 'classroom practice and develop consistently good teaching and learning'. Ofsted stress that this area will have enhanced attention in future inspections, with far more 'inspector time' being spent in classrooms observing lessons. There is further emphasis on the importance of linking a broad, balanced and relevant curriculum with increased pupil motivation and better outcomes.

High-quality teaching is further emphasized in judging the overall effectiveness of a school: 'Similarly, the quality of teaching is critical to securing good progress for pupils and we believe an overall judgment of "good" for the school would require teaching to be good.'

The proposals plan to judge the quality of teaching on six key areas, which focus on:

- teachers having high expectations and ability to motivate pupils
- teachers setting challenging tasks
- teachers' subject knowledge
- teachers carefully assessing pupils' progress
- supporting the needs of all pupils, including those with SEN
- the effective teaching of reading and skills in literacy.

These areas of focus reflect Ofsted's agenda in terms of effective teaching and provide a template for teaching an outstanding lesson for inspection.

## Ten tips for an outstanding lesson

The head teacher has a key role in creating the climate for outstanding teaching. The leadership of a school can provide the environment for everyone to strive towards the very best standards of teaching and learning. This includes ensuring appropriate resources (including support staff), developing an atmosphere of trust, an ambitious agenda and a culture where creativity and risk-taking is encouraged: 'High-quality leadership is essential to promote, support and sustain the drive to perfect teaching and maximise learning in schools' (Twenty Outstanding Primary Schools in Challenging Circumstances).

The head teacher can also support outstanding teaching by developing the skills of teachers. This may include the professional discussion of the theory of learning styles, multiple intelligences and personalised learning. The encouragement of kinaesthetic lessons and outdoor learning should be part of the educational philosophy of a successful school. There is no one approach which will ensure a teacher will deliver an outstanding lesson but the following strategies can underpin outstanding teaching. Very effective lessons may well include:

- an exciting introduction which focuses attention and excites pupils and sets the scene
- progression from one body of knowledge to the next step building on prior learning
- clear expectations based on challenge for every pupil
- knowing every pupil as an individual
- relationships based on mutual respect
- teaching methods matched to the content and pupils
- buzz factor - which enthuse and surprise pupils and create interest
- pace - teaching styles that move the lesson along maintaining interest
- dialogue - discussion and questioning to ensure everyone is involved and understands
- great ending - which helps pupils to reflect on what was learned, celebrates achievement and identifies the next steps.

**In conclusion:-**

Outstanding teaching is hard to define but school leaders can create the climate and environment for excellent teaching to thrive. Sometimes it is more important to focus on outcomes rather than process and a key point is for head teachers to celebrate diversity in teaching styles.

Outstanding teaching can involve using tactile activity, an activity that encourages discussion, some individual interaction with the teacher, a visual stimulus, a written stimulus and a creative stimulus, with the needs of pupils at the core of every lesson. It is important to have a school structure in which every pupil is valued, motivated and confident and in which teachers feel supported and able to innovate and take risks.

## Article 7: Teaching is Not About Us

*Professor Joe Martin*

If we ever have the pleasure of meeting each other, whether it be at an education conference, a teacher workshop, or in a classroom, other than my size (I stand only 5'-6"), you'll notice that I would have adorn two bright red bracelets – one on each wrist. I never take them off. Both are bands I specifically created for a pre-determined purpose: to keep me focused on what's most important when it comes to building my character as a teacher. One band reads "integrity" and the other reads "it's not about me". I started wearing these bands about two years ago, and I haven't taken them off since. They serve as a constant reminder of the following.

1. No matter how difficult my job as a teacher becomes, I must always be a man of my word; do the right thing when no one's looking; and do things for God's approval, not people's.
2. I must always remember that I became a teacher to serve others, not myself, and to always do what's in the best interest of my students.

Why do I refuse to take off my bands, even in the shower (that's probably too much information)? Because I think it's so easy to compromise when things around us get a little uncomfortable. Personally, I believe a little compromise in character invites a little corrosion in character; and I believe a little corrosion of character leads to the corruption of character. And in our profession, I don't believe we can afford neither corrosion nor corruption of character; therefore, I try not to compromise my integrity.

I am well aware of the countless number of challenges we face as both new and veteran teachers. I get dozens of requests to visit, speak, train, and consult with school districts all over the country each year, and sometimes the professional challenges of our job seem insurmountable.

But as I once told a good friend of mine, I've never faced a problem where humbling myself and honoring others have ever gotten me into trouble. I believe in teaching and working with integrity and taking the focus off of our problems and focusing our attention on the future of our students. I know this is easier said than done in a school system that's plagued with bureaucratic red tapeism, little or no support, sometimes incompetent leadership, and often apathetic parents.

However, I believe when we face our creator when our time on earth has expired, and he asks, "What did you do with the children I placed under your care as a teacher"? I don't believe God will accept any of the "logical" excuses we often use to justify a less than 100% commitment to excellence in the lives of our students.

So I want you to ask yourself some of the same tough questions I ask myself when it comes to my commitment to teaching:

1. Am I part of the problem or the solution?
2. Do I focus on the obstacles on my job or the opportunities?
3. Do I make excuses or do I set a positive example for others?
4. Do colleagues and students see me as being full of enthusiasm or full of ego?

If we're honest with ourselves, we know the true answers to these questions. That means either we can keep doing what we're doing, so that we can keep getting the same results or we can choose to change our school by changing our approach and our attitude. The choice is yours. Teach with passion, and remember to practice what you teach.

## Article 8: Teaching is one thing. Learning is another

Teaching and learning are two different processes. Sometimes this fact gets overlooked in today's high-pressured educational environment. I am concerned that teacher's are so "under the gun" to "cover the curriculum" that they are becoming more and more stressed when test results do not demonstrate their hard work. If anything the tests results point to the fact that many students are totally disengaged in the learning process.

Teaching and learning are very different. Teaching is conveying information. Learning requires some kind of engagement of the student in the process of receiving the information. I am reminded of the time I asked my accountant to explain to me why my tax bill was so much higher than it had been the year before as I was sure that my paycheck hadn't gotten any higher. He responded by saying "we have already been over this Joyce".

I then explained to him that he was simply going to have to go back over it again because I still did not understand. His attitude reflects some of what I have seen in many dedicated and well-meaning educators, on my visits to schools all over the country when they express their frustration that their students do not seem to be learning.

Some seem to feel like saying "what do you mean you don't know this, I taught it therefore you must have learned it." They are so focused on teaching, especially teaching for the next of many standardized tests, they cannot believe that their students aren't learning. The learning process is an interactive exchange.

It requires an even exchange between those who are teaching and those who are suppose to be learning. My accountant thought that he had taught me the intricacies of taxation codes. He seemed offended that I had the nerve not to learn what he had taught. I must confess, I feel somewhat inadequate in the area of finances, taxes etc.

It is not my long suit but I am smart enough to know I must understand what is happening financially or I will be out of business quite quickly. There is however, a big difference between knowing that I need to know something and actually understanding new concepts and information. His comments triggered my insecurities and sort of hurt my feelings. Consequently I shared my feelings with some friends. Their responses were unanimous---get another accountant. I was shocked. They explained that I was paying him, not just to crunch numbers; computer programs will do that for no monthly charge. I was paying him a substantial fee to make sure I understood the numbers. They said that it was his job to explain the numbers until I understood. In their judgment his impatience was unacceptable.

Yet, his response to my request for further explanation reflects the frustration of some educators who are so pressed to cover the curriculum that they get angry when the students don't learn. Like my accountant who understands numbers inside and out, most teachers did not have trouble learning anything they are teaching. We sometimes forget what it feels like to have to struggle to learn something, especially something that doesn't seem to have anything to do with our life.

You teach your hearts out. Then the test scores come and you are devastated when the results do not reflect your genuine efforts. The lawmakers and high level administrators who make the policies requiring these tests have forgotten to ask some critical questions "Are they (the students) getting it?", "Are they able to relate to what they are learning?" The emphasis on testing takes away from the emphasis on learning.

I can't emphasize enough how important the person-to-person connection is to the learning process. Times are very different for children today and many parents are too busy or seemingly unconcerned to support their children's learning process. Without that parental support, teachers are sometimes pressed into the role of the only adult in a child's life that cares what happens if the child does not learn. Making a strong positive personal connection with particularly difficult, highly unmotivated students is absolutely essential to success.

You will save a great deal of personal energy by learning strategies for laying more emphasis on the teaching process itself, and a little less on what we are teaching or the fact that many parents aren't helping their children learn. The following suggestions may help you stay focused on the difference between teaching and learning. They can help prevent the frustration and subsequent fatigue that comes when you've taught your heart out and the results do not reflect your efforts.

Keeping the focus on the learning process

Get to know your students personally.

Find out (integrate it into a lesson) what they really care about.

Tell them why you care about what you are teaching.

Tell them that learning will make them feel smart even if they have to learn something that seems irrelevant to their lives. Everyone wants to feel smart.

Check in with them often in the course of a lesson. Ask them: Are you with me? Tell me what I just said. Does this make sense? what do you not get? How can you use this information?

Remind them that working to learn is necessary for everyone. Some have to work harder than others to learn certain things but everyone has to work.

Give them an opportunity to teach what they have learned.

Praise even the smallest progress.

Cheer them on.

Acknowledge their feelings. They do not have to like learning. It may be genuinely boring or confusing to them. That's OK. Tell them, "You don't have to like it." "You do have to do it." And you can.

Ask them to make you proud.

Some of the most unmotivated students will learn just to help you out when they wouldn't do it for themselves.

Keep moving. Walk around. Make constant eye contact.

Try to make it fun.

Take care of yourself. Your personal energy is finite. Don't spend it on things you can't control and be sure to renew it daily by spending some time some time doing the things you love.

Remind yourself that you are doing the hardest and most important work on the planet. Pat yourself on the back.

## Article 9: Believe in what you teach

*Professor Joe Martin*

As teachers, we know all too well how tough it is to keep up our energy levels to teach students who sometimes don't want to learn. I've even heard students describe us (teachers) as being "just a speed bump to a grade". It is true that more and more students are not mastering the necessary basic skills to succeed. It's also true that more and more students are taking their education for granted and not respecting the process and institution of learning. However, these obstacles also offer us an opportunity to make a huge impact on our students.

One of the cardinal rules of teaching is that students will not believe in you until you first believe in them and in what you're teaching them. As discouraging as some students' attitudes are, nothing should negate the fact that as teachers, we have an opportunity to take a closed mind and replace it with an open one. In essence, that's our number one priority...to get students to think Your class gives you a great opportunity to get students to open their minds and challenge themselves beyond their limits. You're not only teaching them basic skills, you're teaching them "life skills" – skills that will impact them well beyond the classroom. Unfortunately, if you don't believe this is true, neither will your students.

To get yourself in the right mindset for teaching your class, skim through your learning objectives. Then ask yourself, "Would I have benefited from this material as a student?" If not, then you definitely should not be teaching the subject, because you will have no conviction in the classroom. And we've all heard the saying, "When it comes to children, you can't kid a kid". The same is true about students. Students can detect an insincere teacher faster than a fake I.D. However, if you truly believe that the knowledge and information contained in your class has or would have proven to be beneficial to you as a student, then ask yourself, "How?" The rest is simple; simply take your conviction and passion, and then put it into the curriculum and class discussions. The fact of the matter is, students will only care about your class to the degree to which you do. If you don't care about a thing, that "thing" can become a burden on you. Likewise, if you cc a "thing" for the wrong reasons, you become a burden on others. And quite frankly, if you don't care, you shouldn't teach.

'Teachers should be role models' - speech by Dr A.P.J. Abdul Kalam (on the occassion of Teachers' Day 2003)

**Teachers should be role models**

Dear listeners of All India Radio and teachers, my greetings to all of you.

I am talking to you on the special occasion of Teachers' day. On this day, we gratefully remember the great educationist Dr Sarvepalli Radhakrishnan, whose dream was that "teachers should be the best minds in the country". Hence, Teachers' day is very important for all our people, for our students and even for all the parents, as the teachers lay the foundation for creating enlightened citizens for the nation. On this day, I would like to recall three teachers who helped me in shaping my life.

To begin with I am going to talk to you about my father Janab Avul Pakir Jainulabdeen, as a teacher. My father taught me a great lesson when I was a young boy. What was that lesson? It was just after India got Independence. At that time Panchayat board elections took place at Rameswaram. My father was elected as Panchayat Board member and on the same day he was also elected the president of the Rameswaram Panchayat Board. Rameswaram was a beautiful island with a population of 30,000. At that time they elected my father as Panchayat Board president not because he belonged to a particular religion or a particular caste or spoke a particular language or for his economic status. He was elected only on the basis of his nobility of mind and for being a good human being. Dear listeners, I would like to narrate one incident that took place on the day he was elected the president of the Panchayat Board.

I was at that time studying in school. Those days we did not have electricity and we used to study under ration kerosene lamps. I was reading the lessons loudly and I heard a knock on the door. We never used to lock the door in Rameswaram in those days. Somebody opened the door, came in and asked me where my father was? I told him that father had gone for the evening namaz. Then he said, I have brought something for him, can I keep it here? Since my father had gone for namaz, I shouted for my mother to get her permission to receive the item. Since she was also performing the namaz there was no response. I asked the person to leave the item on the cot. After that I continued my studies.

I used to learn by reading aloud in my younger days. I was reading loud and fully concentrating on my studies. At that time my father came in and saw a tambulam kept in the cot. He asked me "What is this? Who has given that?" I told him, "Somebody came and has kept this for you". He opened the cover of the tambulam and found there was a costly dhoti, angawastram, some fruits and some sweets and he could see the slip that the person had left behind. I was the youngest child of my father, he really loved me and I also loved him a lot. He was upset at the sight of the gifts.

That was the first time I saw him very angry and also that was the first time I had got a thorough beating from him. I got frightened and started weeping. My mother embraced and consoled me. Then my father came and touched my shoulder lovingly with affection and advised me not to receive any gift without his permission. He quoted an Islamic Hadith, which states that, "When the Almighty appoints a person to a position, He takes care of his provision. If a person takes anything beyond that, it is an illegal gain". Then he told me that it is not a good habit. A gift is always accompanied by some purpose and a gift is a dangerous thing. It is like touching a snake and getting the poison in turn. This lesson stands out always in my mind even when I am in my seventies. This incident, taught me a very valuable lesson for my life. It is deeply embedded in my mind.

I would like also to mention the writings in Manu Smriti which states that "By accepting gifts the divine light in the person gets extinguished". Manu warns every individual against accepting gifts for the reason that it places the acceptor under an obligation in favour of the person who gave the gift and ultimately it results in making a person to do things which are not permitted according to law.

I am sharing this thought, with all of you, particularly the young ones, do not be carried away by any gift which comes with a purpose and through which one loses his personality. Do you think, you can follow this in your life? I will be very happy if you can practice this sincerely.

When I think of my second teacher, I am reminded of my childhood days when I was studying in 8th class at the age of 13. I had a teacher, Shri Siva Subramania Iyer. He was one of the very good teachers in our school. All of us loved to attend his class. One day he was teaching about a bird's flight. He drew a diagram of a bird on the blackboard depicting the wings, tail and the body structure with the head. He explained how birds create the lift and fly. He also explained to us how they change direction while flying. For nearly 25 minutes he gave the lecture with various information such as lift, drag, how the birds fly in a formation of 10, 20 or 30. At the end of the class, he wanted to know whether we understood how birds fly. I said, I did not understand. When I said this, the teacher asked the other students whether they understood or not. Many students said that they also did not understand. He did not get upset by our response since he was a committed teacher.

Our teacher said that he would take all of us to the sea shore. That evening the whole class was at the sea shore of Rameswaram. We enjoyed the roaring sea waves knocking at the sandy hills in the pleasant evening. Birds were flying with sweet chirping voice. He showed the sea birds in formations of 10 to 20 in number. We saw the marvellous formations of birds with a purpose and we were all amazed. He showed us the birds and asked us to see that when the birds fly, what they looked like. We saw the wings flapping. He asked us to look at the tail portion with the combination of flapping wings and twisting tail. We noticed closely and found that the birds in that condition flew in the direction they desired. Then he asked us a question, "Where the engine is and how it is powered"?

The bird is powered by its own life and the motivation of what it wants. All these things were explained to us within fifteen minutes. We all understood the dynamics from this practical example. How nice it was. Our teacher was a great teacher; he could give us a theoretical lesson coupled with a live practical example available in nature. This is real teaching. I am sure many of the teachers in schools and colleges will follow this example.

For me, it was not merely an understanding of how a bird flies. The bird's flight entered into me and created a special feeling. From that evening, I thought that my future study has to be with reference to flight and flight systems. I am saying this because my teacher's teaching and the event that I witnessed decided my future career.

Then one evening after the classes, I asked the teacher, "Sir, please tell me, how to progress further in learning all about flight." He patiently explained to me that I should complete 8th class, and then go to high school, and then I should go to engineering college that may lead to education on flight. If I complete all my education with excellence, I might do something connected with flight sciences. This advice and the bird flying exercise given by my teacher, really gave me a goal and a mission for my life. When I went to college, I took physics. When I went to engineering in Madras Institute of Technology, I took aeronautical engineering.

Thus my life was transformed as a rocket engineer, aerospace engineer and technologist. That one incident of my teacher teaching the lesson, showing the visual live example proved to be a turning point in my life which eventually shaped my profession.

A student during his school life upto 10+2 spends 25,000 hours in the school campus. His life is more influenced by the teachers and the school environment. Therefore, the school must have the best of teachers with an ability to, teach and the love for teaching and building moral qualities. Teachers should become role models. Similarly, the student must be alert to build himself with best of qualities and to get ignited with a vision for his or her future life.

I would like to share with you another experience with my teacher Prof. Satish Dhawan. First, I worked in Delhi with the Ministry of Defence. Later I joined the Defence Research and Development Organisation (DRDO) in 1958 at the Aeronautical Development Establishment at Bangalore. There with the advice of the Director, I took up the development of hovercraft. Hovercraft design needed the development of a ducted contra-rotating propeller for creating a smooth flow balancing the torques. I did not know how to design a contra-rotating propeller though I knew how to design a conventional propeller. Some of my friends told me that I could approach Prof. Satish Dhawan of the Indian Institute of Science, who was well known for his aeronautical research, for help.

I took permission from my Director Dr Mediratta and went to Prof Dhawan who was sitting in a small room in the Indian Institute of Science with a lot of books in the background and a blackboard on the wall. Prof Dhawan asked me what the problem was that I wanted to discuss. I explained the problem.. He told me that it was really a challenging task and he would teach me the design if I attended his classes in IISc between 2 pm to 3 pm on all Saturdays for the next six weeks.

He was a visionary teacher. He prepared the schedule for the entire course and wrote it on the black board. He also gave me the reference material and books I should read before I start attending the course. I considered, this as a great opportunity and I started attending the discussion and started meeting him regularly. Before commencing each meeting, he would ask critical questions and assess my understanding of the subject. That was for the first time that I realized how a good teacher prepares himself for teaching with meticulous planning and prepares the student for acquisition of knowledge. This process continued for the next six weeks. I got the capability for designing the contra-rotating propeller. Prof Dhawan told me that I was ready for developing the contra-rotating propeller for a given hovercraft configuration. That was the time I realized that

Prof Dhawan was not only a teacher but also a fantastic development engineer of aeronautical systems.

Later during the critical phases of testing, Prof Dhawan was with me to witness the test and find solutions to the problems. After reaching the smooth test phase, the contra-rotating propeller went through 50 hours of continuous testing. Prof Dhawan witnessed the test himself and congratulated me. That was a great day for me when I saw the contra rotating propeller designed by my team performing to the mission requirement in the hovercraft. However, at that time, I did not realize that Prof Dhawan would become chairman, ISRO and that I would get the opportunity to work with him as a project director in the development of the satellite launch vehicle SLV-3 for injecting the Rohini satellite into the orbit. Nature has its own way to link the student's dream and real life later.

This was the first design in my career which gave me the confidence to design many complex aerospace systems in future. The hovercraft could fly just above the ground level carrying two passengers. I was the first pilot for this hovercraft and I could control and maneuver the vehicle in any direction. Through this project I learnt the techniques of designing and developing the contra-rotating propeller. Above all, I learnt that in a project, problems will always crop up; we should not allow problems to be our masters but we should defeat the problems. Then success will sparkle.

The three teachers in my life; what did they give me? In an integrated way it can be said, that any enlightened human being can be created by three unique characteristics. One is moral value system. That I got from my father the hard way. Secondly, the teacher becoming a role model. Not only does the student learn, but the teacher shapes his life with great dreams and aims. Finally, the education and learning process has to culminate in the creation of professional capability leading to confidence and will power to make a design, to make a product, to make a system, bravely combating many problems. What a fortune and blessing I had from my three teachers.

Among the listeners, there may be many parents, many teachers and a large number of students. Every one of us in this planet creates a page in human history irrespective of who he/she is. I realize my experience is a small dot in human life, but that dot has a life and light. This light, let it light many lamps.

My best wishes to all of you on this occasion of Teachers' day.

# Quotes on Teachers and Teaching

1. The task of the excellent teacher is to stimulate "apparently ordinary" people to unusual effort. The tough problem is not in identifying winners: it is in making winners out of ordinary people.

   *- K. Patricia Cross*

2. Let us think of education as the means of developing our greatest abilities, because in each of us there is a private hope and dream which, fulfilled, can be translated into benefit for everyone and greater strength of the nation.

   *– John F. Kennedy*

3. Your role as a leader is even more important than you might imagine. You have the power to help people become winners.

   *-Ken Blanchard*

4. A teacher affects eternity; he can never tell where his influence stops.

   *-Henry Adams*

5. If you want to live more, you must master the art of appreciating the little everyday blessings of life. This is not altogether a golden world but there are countless gleams of gold to be discovered in it.

   *-Henry Alfred Porter*

6. Don't limit yourself. Many people limit themselves to what they think they can do. You can go as far as your mind lets you. What you believe, you can achieve.

   *- Mary Kay Ash*

7. One never notices what has been done; one can only see what remains to be done.

   *Marie Curie*

8. The best teachers teach from the heart, not from the book.

   *-Author Unknown*

9. I am indebted to my father for living, but to my teacher for living well.

   *-Alexander the Great*

10. It's easy to make a buck. It's a lot tougher to make a difference.

*-Tom Brokaw*

11. Teacher appreciation makes the world of education go around.

*- Helen Peters*

12. The dream begins with a teacher who believes in you, who tugs and pushes and leads you to the next plateau, sometimes poking you with a sharp stick called "truth".

*-Dan Rather*

13. He who opens a school door, closes a prison.

*-Victor Hugo*

14. What the teacher is, is more important than what he teaches.

*-Karl Menninger*

15. A truly special teacher is very wise, and sees tomorrow in every child's eyes.

*Author Unknown*

16. Ideal teachers are those who use themselves as bridges over which they invite their students to cross, then having facilitated their crossing, joyfully collapse, encouraging them to create bridges of their own.

*- Nikos Kazantzakis*

17. Learning is finding out what we already know. Doing is demonstrating that you know it. Teaching is reminding others that they know just as well as you. You are all learners, doers, and teachers.

*- Richard Bach*

18. A teacher who can arouse a feeling for one single good action, for one single good poem, accomplishes more than he who fills our memory with rows and rows of natural objects, classified with name and form."

*- Johann Wolfgang von Goethe*

19. What a teacher writes on the blackboard of life can never be erased.

*-Author Unknown*

20. Discover wildlife: be a teacher!

*~Author Unknown*

21. Summer vacation is the time when parents realize that teachers are grossly underpaid.

*-Author Unknown*

22. A teacher takes a hand, opens a mind, and touches a heart.

*-Author Unknown*

23. Treat people as if they were what they ought to be and you help them become what they are capable of becoming.

*- Goethe*

24. Once children learn how to learn, nothing is going to narrow their mind. The essence of teaching is to make learning contagious, to have one idea spark another.

*- Marva Collins*

25. In education it isn't how much you have committed to memory or even how much you know. It's being able to differentiate between what you do know and what you don't. It's knowing where to go to find out what you need to know and it's knowing how to use the information you get.

*-William Feather*

26. None of us got where we are solely by pulling ourselves up by our bootstraps. We got here because somebody - a parent, a teacher, an Ivy League crony or a few nuns - bent down and helped us pick up our boots.

*- Thurgood Marshall*

27. Teaching is not a lost art, but the regard for it is a lost tradition.

*- Jacques Barzun*

28. In teaching you cannot see the fruit of a day's work. It is invisible and remains so, maybe for twenty years.

*-Jacques Barzun*

29. No one who achieves success does so without acknowledging the help of others. The wise and confident acknowledge this help with gratitude.

*-Author Unknown*

30. They may forget what you said but they will never forget how you made them feel.

*- Carol Buchner*

31. We often take for granted the very things that most deserve our gratitude.

*- Cynthia Ozick*

32. Often, when I am reading a good book, I stop and thank my teacher. That is, I used to, until she got an unlisted number.

*-Author Unknown*

33. The teacher who is indeed wise does not bid you to enter the house of his wisdom but rather leads you to the threshold of your mind.

*-Khalil Gibran*

34. The hardest arithmetic to master is that which enables us to count our blessings.

*- Eric Hoffer*

35. Good teaching is one-fourth preparation and three-fourths pure theatre.

*-Gail Godwin*

36. The only people with whom you should try to get even are those who have helped you.

*-John E. Southard*

37. If a seed of a lettuce will not grow, we do not blame the lettuce. Instead, the fault lies with us for not having nourished the seed properly.

*- Buddhist proverb*

38. The great end of education is to discipline rather than to furnish the mind; to train it to the use of its own powers rather than to fill it with the accumulation of others.

*- Tyron Edwards*

39. Good teaching is more a giving of right questions than a giving of right answers.

*-Josef Albers*

40. Every truth has four corners: as a teacher I give you one corner, and it is for you to find the other three.

*- Confucius*

41. I've seen and met angels wearing the disguise of ordinary people living ordinary lives.

*-Tracy Chapman*

42. Feeling gratitude and not expressing it is like wrapping a present and not giving it.

*- William Arthur Ward*

43. Thought flows in terms of stories -- stories about events, stories about people, and stories about intentions and achievements. The best teachers are the best storytellers. We learn in the form of stories.

*- Frank Smith*

44. A teacher who is attempting to teach without inspiring the pupil with a desire to learn is hammering on cold iron.

*- Horace Mann*

45. No matter how he may think himself accomplished, when he sets out to learn a new language, science or the bicycle, he has entered a new realm as truly as if he were a child newly born into the world.

*- Frances Willard*

46. We should not teach children the sciences but give them a taste for them.

*- Jean Jacques Rousseau*

47. Much education today is monumentally ineffective. All too often we are giving young people cut flowers when we should be teaching them to grow their own plants.

*- John Gardner*

48. The teacher who is indeed wise does not bid you to enter the house of wisdom but rather leads you to the threshold of your mind. -

*Kahlil Gibran*

49. A very wise old teacher once said: "I consider a day's teaching wasted if we do not all have one hearty laugh." He meant that when people laugh together, they cease to be young and old, master and pupils, jailer and prisoners. They become a single group of human beings enjoying its existence.

*- Gilbert Highet*

50. To ensure that your work is also a play, I recommend that you develop a personal mission statement. This will help you find what it is to enjoy so much that you lose track of time when you're doing it.

*- Ken Blanchard*

51. Each man must look to himself to teach him the meaning of life. It is not something discovered. It is something moulded.

*- Antoine De Saint-Exupery*

52. It is not what is poured into a student that counts but what is planted.

*- Linda Conway*

53. The greatest sign of a success for a teacher...is to be able to say, "The children are now working as if I did not exist.

*- Maria Montessori*

54. There is in every child a painstaking teacher so skillful that he obtains identical results in all children in all parts of the world. The only language men ever speak perfectly is the one they learn in babyhood, when no one teaches them anything.

*-Maria Montessori*

55. We learn by example and by direct experience because there are real limits to the adequacy of verbal instruction.

*- Malcom Gladwell*

56. You must train the children to their studies in a playful manner and without any air of constraint with the further object of discerning more readily the natural bent of their respective characters.

*– Plato*

57. Education is not the filling of a pail but the lighting of a fire.

*-William Butler Yeats*

58. If a child is to keep alive his inborn sense of wonder, he needs the companionship of at least one adult who can share it, rediscovering with him the joy, the excitement, and the mystery of the world we live in.

*-Rachel Carlson*

59. I challenge you to make your life like a masterpiece. I challenge you to join the ranks of those people, who live what they teach, who walk their talk.

*- Anthony Robbins*

60. A hundred years from now, it will not matter what kind of car I drove, what kind of house I lived in, how much money I had in the bank...but the world may be a better place because I made a difference in the life of a child.

*- Forest Witcraft*

●●

# Shlokas on Gurus

अखण्डमण्डलाकारं व्याप्तं येन चराचरम्।
तत्पदं दर्शितं येन तस्मै श्रीगुरवे नमः।।

akhandamandalaakaaran vyaaptan yena charaacharam
tatpadan darshitan yena tasmai sri-gurave namah

**Meaning:** Salutation to the noble Guru, who has made it possible to realise the state which pervades the entire cosmos, everything animate and inanimate.

अज्ञानतिमिरान्धस्य ज्ञानाञ्जनशलकया।
चक्षुरुन्मीलितं येन तस्मै श्रीगुरवे नमः।।

ajnanatimirandhasya jnananjanasalakaya
chakshurunmilitam yena tasmai sri-gurave namah

**Meaning:** Salutation to the noble Guru, who has opened the eyes blinded by darkness of ignorance with the collyrium-stick of knowledge.

गुरुर्ब्रह्मा गुरुर्विष्णुः गुरुर्देवो महेश्वरः।
गुरुरेव परंब्रह्म तस्मै श्रीगुरवे नमः।।

gurubrahma guruvishnuh gururdevo maheshvarah
gurureva parambrahma tasmai sri-gurave namah

**Meaning:** Salutation to the noble Guru, who is Brahma, Vishnu and Maheswara, the direct Parabrahma, the Supreme Reality.

स्थावरं जंगमं व्याप्तं यत्किंचित्सचराचरन्।
तत्पदं दर्शितं येन तस्मै श्रीगुरवे नमः।।

sthaavaram jangamam vyaaptam yatkinchitsacharaacharam
tatpadam darshitam yena tasmai sri-gurave namah

**Meaning:** Salutation to the noble Guru, who has made it possible to realise Him, by whom all that is – sentient and insentient, movable and immovable is pervaded.

चिन्मयं व्यापियत्सर्वं त्रैलोक्यं सचराचरम्।
तत्पदं दर्शितं येन तस्मै श्रीगुरवे नमः।।

chinmayam vyaapiyatsarvane trailokyan sacharaacharam
tatpadam darshitam yena tasmai sri-gurave namah

**Meaning:** Salutation to the noble Guru, who has made it possible to realise Him pervades everything, sentient and insentient, in all three worlds.

त्सर्वश्रुतिशिरोरत्नविराजित पदाम्बुजः।
वेदान्ताम्बुजसूर्योयः तस्मै श्रीगुरवे नमः।।

tsarvashrutishiroratnaviraajita padaambujah
vedaantaambujasuuryoyah tasmai sri-gurave namah

**Meaning:** Salutation to the noble guru, whose lotus feet are radient with (the luster of) the crest jewel of all srutis and who is the sun that causes the vendanta lotus (knowledge) to blossom.

चैतन्यः शाश्वतःशान्तो व्योमातीतो निरंजनः।
बिन्दुनाद कलातीतः तस्मै श्रीगुरवे नमः।।

chaitanyah shaashvatahshaanto vyomaatiito niranjanah
bindunaada kalaatiitah tasmai sri-gurave namah

**Meaning:** Salutation to the noble Guru, who is the ever effulgent, eternal, peaceful, beyond space, immaculate, and beyond the manifest and unmanifest.

ज्ञानशक्तिसमारूढः तत्त्वमालाविभूषितः।
भुक्तिमुक्तिप्रदाता च तस्मै श्रीगुरवे नमः॥

dnyaanashaktisamsasuudhah tattvamaalavibhuushitah
bhuktimuktipradaataa cha tasmai sri-gurave namah

**Meaning:** Salutation to that noble Guru, who is established in the power of knowledge, adorned with the garland of various principles and is the bestower of prosperity and liberation.

अनेकजन्मसंप्राप्त कर्मबन्धविदाहिने।
आत्मज्ञानप्रदानेन तस्मै श्रीगुरवे नमः॥

anekajanmasamprapta karmabandhavidaahine
aatmadnyaanapradaanena tasmai sri-gurave namah

**Meaning:** Salutation to the noble Guru, who by bestowing the knowledge of the Self burns up the bondage created by accumulated actions of innumerable births.

शोषणं भवसिन्धोश्च ज्ञापणं सारसंपदः।
गुरोः पादोदकं सम्यक् तस्मै श्रीगुरवे नमः।

shoshanam bhavasindhoshcha gyapanan saarasampadah
guroh paadodakam samyak tasmai sri-gurave namah

**Meaning:** Salutation to the noble Guru, by washing whose feet, the ocean of transmigration, endless sorrows is completely dried up and the Supreme wealth is revealed.

न गुरोरधिकं तत्त्वं न गुरोरधिकं तपः।
तत्त्वज्ञानात्परं नास्ति तस्मै श्रीगुरवे नमः॥

na guroradhikam tattvam na guroradhikam tapah
tattvadnyaanaatparam naasti tasmai sri-gurave namah

**Meaning:** Salutation to the noble Guru, beyond whom there is no higher truth, there is no higher penance and there is nothing higher attainable than the true knowledge.

मन्नाथः श्रीजगन्नाथः मद्गुरुः श्रीजगद्गुरुः।
मदात्मा सर्वभूतात्मा तस्मै श्रीगुरवे नमः।।

mannaathah shrijagannaathah madguruh shrijagadguruh
madaatmaa sarvabhuutaatmaa tasmai sri-gurave namah

**Meaning:** Salutation to the noble Guru, who is my Lord and the Lord of the Universe, my Teacher and the Teacher of the Universe, who is the Self in me and the Self in all beings.

गुरुरादिरनादिश्च गुरुः परमदैवतम्।
गुरोः परतरं नास्ति तस्मै श्रीगुरवे नमः।।

gururaadiranaadishcha guruh paramadaivatam
guroh parataram naasti tasmai sri-gurave namah

**Meaning:** Salutation to the noble Guru, who is both the beginning and beginningless, who is the Supreme Deity than whom there is none superior.

त्वमेव माता च पिता त्वमेव, त्वमेव बन्धुश्च सखा त्वमेव।
त्वमेव विद्या द्रविणं त्वमेव, त्वमेव सर्वं मम देव देव।।

tvameva maataa cha pitaa tvameva, tvameva bandhushcha sakhaa tvameva
tvameva vidyaa dravinam tvameva, tvameva sarvam mama deva deva

Meaning: (Oh Guru!) You are my mother and father; you are my brother and companion; you alone are knowledge and wealth. O Lord, you are everything to me.

poojamoolam guroh padam
mantramoolam guror vaakyam
moksha moolam guru krupa.

**Meaning:** The guru's form is the best to meditate upon; the guru's feet are the best for worship; the guru's word is the mantra; the guru's grace is the root of liberation.

kevalam jnaana murthim

dhvandhvaa theetham gagana sadhrisham

tathvam asyaadi lakshyam

ekam nithyam vimalam achalam

sarvadhee saakshi bhutham

bhavaatheetham thriguna rahitham

sadhgurum tham namaami.

**Meaning:** This sloka tries to describe the qualities of a true guru. A real guru has the following qualities. He experiences the supreme bliss of Brahmaananda (transcedental divine bliss). He enjoys and confers changeless supreme happiness. He is beyond space and time (there is nothing higher than him). He is the embodiment of wisdom which is the basis for all types of knowledge.

He transcends the pair of opposites (such as happiness and sorrow, gain and loss). He is more omnipresent than space itself. He is the very embodiment of the divine principle, which is the inner meaning of the four great pronouncements Prajnaanam Brahma, Aham Brahmasmi, Thath Thvam Asi and Ayam Aathma Brahma.

He is one without a second (ekam). He never changes under any circumstances (nithyam). He is without any type of impurity (vimalam). He is steady and motionless (achalam). He is the witness of everything. He transcends mental comprehension and verbal explanation. He is beyond the three gunas (sathva, rajas and thamas). I offer my humble salutations to such a guru who possesses all these qualities.

gurave sarva lokaanaam

bhishaje bhava roginaam

nidhaye sarva vidyaanaam

dakshina moorthaye namaha

**Meaning:** I salute Dakshina Moorthy (Shiva in Guru form) who is the guru of all the worlds, the one who cures the disease of worldly existence and who is wealth of all knowledge.

shruthi smruthi puraanaam
aalayam karunaalayam
namaami bhagavat paadam
shankaram loka shankaram.

**Meaning:** I prostrate before Shanakara Bhagavatpada who is the house of all knowledge, the shrutis, smrutis and puranas (all the vedic texts).

namastutey vyaasa vishaala buddhe
phullaaravinda yatapatra netra
yena twaya bhaarata tailapoorna
prajwaalito gyaana mayah pradeepaha

**Meaning:** Salutations unto thee, O Vyasa of broad intellect and with eyes large like petals of full blown lotuses, by whom the lamp of knowledge filled with the oil of Mahabharata has been lighted.

namah sree sai naathaaya
mohatandra vinaashine
gurave buddhi bodhaaya
bodha maatra swaroopine

**Meaning:** I worship Lord Sainath, the destroyer of attachment, the guru who preaches discrimination and sharpens the intellect.

poojyaaya raaghavendraaya
sathya dhrama vrataayacha
bhajataam kalpa vrikshaaya
namathaam kaamadhenave

**Meaning:** I prostrate before the venerable guru Raghavendra who is always professing truth and righteousness, the one who is like the kalpavriksha (wish fulfilling tree) and kamadhenu (celestial cow indicating prosperity) to the devotees (meaning he is a boon giver).

# Poems On Teachers

## 1. In Good Hands

In the hands of a gifted teacher
a classroom is a magical place.

In the hands of a gifted teacher
there's a smile on each child's face.

In the hands of a gifted teacher
creative energy is everywhere.

In the hands of a gifted teacher
there's a catalyst who genuinely cares.

In the hands of a gifted teacher
desire and wonder is awakened.

In the hands of a gifted teacher
the educational agenda is shaken.

In the hands of a gifted teacher
self-management skills are modelled.

In the hands of a gifted teacher
the best of reality is bottled.

In the hands of a gifted teacher
gifts and talents are refined.

In the hands of a gifted teacher
the willed future is designed.

- Ultimate Cyan

## 2. Teacher Man

The Teacher Man teaches kids from all over the world
The Teacher Man teaches no matter boy or girl
The Teacher Man teaches Christans, Muslims, and Jews
The Teacher Man teaches those who say 'God I don't believe in you'
The Teacher Man teaches over demands for more recess
The Teacher Man teaches to only demand the best
The Teacher Man teaches Science, reading, and Math
The Teacher Man teaches how to live out of class
The Teacher Man teaches all how to share
The Teacher Man teaches that we all should care
The Teacher Man teaches how to keep an open mind
The Teacher Man teaches with a kick in the behind
The Teacher Man teaches there are lessons in life
The Teacher Man teaches how to overcome strife
The Teacher Man teaches there's nothing wrong with a hug
The Teacher Man teaches the world changes with love
The Teacher Man teaches the rich and the poor
The Teacher Man teaches those who are ready for more
The Teacher Man teaches how to look someone in the eye
The Teacher Man teaches how to accept someone in their cry
The Teacher Man teaches in more than one tongue
The Teacher Man teaches how to make working hard fun
The Teacher Man teaches all the colors of the land
But, most important of all, he teaches we should take a stand
Take a stand, take a stand, for what you believe
Take a stand, take a stand, and you will be free
Take a stand, take a stand, for the least of the least
Take such stand man, and you will find peace
He's the Teacher Man

- Ary bolanos

### 3. When you thought I wasn't looking

When you thought I wasn't looking, you displayed my first report,
and I wanted to do another.

When you thought I wasn't looking, you fed a stray cat,
and I thought it was good to be kind to animals.

When you thought I wasn't looking, you gave me a sticker,
and I knew that little things were special things.

When you thought I wasn't looking, you put your arm around me,
and I felt loved.

When you thought I wasn't looking I saw tears come from your eyes,
and I learned that sometimes things hurt – but that it's all right to cry.

When you thought I wasn't looking, you smiled,
and it made me want to look that pretty too.

When you thought I wasn't looking, you cared,
and I wanted to be everything I could be.

When you thought I wasn't looking – I looked...and wanted to say thanks for all
those things you did when you thought I wasn't looking.

– Mary Rita Schilke Korzan

## 4. Whose child is this?

"Whose child is this?" I asked one day
Seeing a little one out at play
"Mine," said the parent with a tender smile
"Mine to keep a little while
To bathe his hands and comb his hair
To tell him what he is to wear
To prepare him that he may always be good
And each day do the things he should.

"Whose child is this?" I asked again
As the door opened and someone came in
"Mine," said the teacher with the same tender smile
"Mine, to keep just for a little while
To teach him how to be gentle and kind
To train and direct his dear little mind
To help him live by every rule
And get the best he can from school."

"Whose child is this?" I ask once more
Just as the little one entered the door
"Ours," said the parent and the teacher as they smiled
And each took the hand of the little child
"Ours to love and train together
Ours this blessed task forever.

- Anonymous

## 5. Why God Made Teachers

When God created teachers,
He gave us special friends
To help us understand His world
And truly comprehend
The beauty and the wonder
Of everything we see,
And become a better person
With each discovery.
When God created teachers,
He gave us special guides
To show us ways in which to grow
So we can all decide
How to live and how to do
What's right instead of wrong,
To lead us so that we can lead
And learn how to be strong.
Why God created teachers,
In His wisdom and His grace,
Was to help us learn to make our world
A better, wiser place.

– Kevin William Huff

## 6. Teachers

Teachers
Paint their minds
and guide their thoughts
Share their achievements
and advise their faults

Inspire a love
of knowledge and truth
As you light the path
Which leads our youth

For our future brightens
with each lesson you teach
Each smile you lengthen
Each goal you help reach
For the dawn of each poet
each philosopher and king
Begins with a Teacher
And the wisdom they bring

– Kevin William Huff

## 7. Poem by Cleo V. Swarat

I dreamed I stood in a studio
And watched two sculptors there,
The clay they used was a young child's mind
And they fashioned it with care.
One was a teacher:
the tools she used were books and music and art;
One was a parent
With a guiding hand and gentle loving heart.
And when at last their work was done,
They were proud of what they had wrought.
For the things they had worked into the child
Could never be sold or bought
And each agreed she would have failed
if she had worked alone.
For behind the parent stood the school,
and behind the teacher stood the home!

– V. Swart

## 8. Poem of gratitude

For teaching children lessons,
to help them as they grow,
Let this gift remind you,
You're the best teacher we know!

- Anonymous

## 9. Poem of gratitude

I chose this special present because I wanted you to know,
That I'm grateful for your hard work in helping me to grow.
For your constant understanding and for always being there,
To tell me I can do it and to show me that you care!

– Anonymous

## 10. The creation of the teacher

The good Lord was creating teachers. It was His sixth day of 'overtime' and He knew that this was a tremendous responsibility, for teachers would touch the lives of so many impressionable young children. An angel appeared to Him and said, "You are taking a long time to figure this one out."

"Yes," said the Lord, "but have you read the specs on this order?"

TEACHER

...must stand above all students, yet be on their level

... must be able to do 180 things not connected with the subject being taught

... must run on coffee and leftovers,

... must communicate vital knowledge to all students daily and be right most of the time

... must have more time for others than for herself/himself

... must have a smile that can endure through pay cuts, problematic children, and worried parents

... must go on teaching when parents question every move and others are not supportive

... must have 6 pairs of hands.

"Six pairs of hands," said the angel, "that's impossible."

"Well," said the Lord, "it is not the hands that are the problem. It is the three pairs of eyes that are presenting the most difficulty."

The angel looked incredulous, "Three pairs of eyes...on a standard model?"

The Lord nodded His head, "One pair can see a student for what he is and not what others have labeled him as. Another pair of eyes is in the back of the teacher's head to see what should not be seen, but what must be known. The eyes in the front are only to look at the child as he/she 'acts out' in order to reflect, "I understand and I still believe in you," without so much as saying a word to the child.

"Lord," said the angel, "this is a very large project and I think you should work on it tomorrow."

"I can't," said the Lord, "for I have come very close to creating something much like myself. I have one that comes to work when he/she is sick.....teaches a class of children that do not want to learn....has a special place in his/her heart for children who are not his/her own.....understands the struggles of those who have difficulty.... never takes the students for granted..."

The angel looked closely at the model the Lord was creating.

"It is too soft-hearted," said the angel.

"Yes," said the Lord, "but also tough, You can not imagine what this teacher can endure or do, if necessary."

"Can this teacher think?" asked the angel.

"Not only think," said the Lord, "but reason and compromise."

The angel came closer to have a better look at the model and ran his finger over the teacher's cheek.

"Well, Lord," said the angel, your job looks fine but there is a leak. I told you that you were putting too much into this model. You can not imagine the stress that will be placed upon the teacher."

The Lord moved in closer and lifted the drop of moisture from the teacher's cheek. It shone and glistened in the light.

"It is not a leak," He said, "It is a tear."

"A tear? What is that?" asked the angel, "What is a tear for?"

The Lord replied with great thought, "It is for the joy and pride of seeing a child accomplish even the smallest task. It is for the loneliness of children who have a hard time to fit in and it is for compassion for the feelings of their parents. It comes from the pain of not being able to reach some children and the disappointment those children feel in themselves. It comes often when a teacher has been with a class for a year and must say good-bye to those students and get ready to welcome a new class."

"My," said the angel, "The tear thing is a great idea...you are a genius!!"

The Lord looked somber, "I didn't put it there."

– Anonymous

# 11. शिक्षक दिवस है पर्व सुनहरा

है आज बहुत हर्षित मन मेरा,
शिक्षक दिवस है पर्व सुनहरा
इस पुलकित पावन अवसर पर,
वंदन करता है मन मेरा।।

आपकी महिमा आपका गौरव
आपका चिंतन आपका ज्ञान।

आपके ही उपदेश वचन
करते हैं सबका कल्याण।।

आपकी गरिमा का क्या बखान करें,
आपके गौरव का कैसे गुणगान करें।
डरती है लेखनी मेरी,
न कहीं कोई यह भूल करे।।

आपने ही त्रिदोष बताए,
सप्तधातुओं से ज्ञान कराया।
'आयुर्वेद' के अष्ट-अंगों से,
आप ही ने तो संज्ञान कराया।।

आयुर्वेद का इतिहास बताकर,
इसके महत्त्व का अहसास कराया।
दर्शन का दृष्टा बनाकर,
आत्मा-परमात्मा का मिलन कराया।।

संस्कृत के संस्कार बताए,
और भाषा का ज्ञान सिखाया।
आयुर्वेदिक चिकित्सा पद्धति से,
'आयर्वेदामृत' जन-जन को पिलाया।।

ऐसे गुरुजन आपको हृदय से वंदन,
इस पुलकित-पावन अवसर पर।
पुनः-पुनः सहस्त्र नमन,
पुनः-पुनः सहस्त्र नमन।।

-डॉ. सुलोचना बगाना

# 12. शिक्षक

कभी सोचता वह,
मध्य नहीं कोई प्रतिबंध,
कभी सखा तो कभी ज्येष्ठ सा,
कभी पित्र सा वह आबंध
वे सदैव मेरे उर-तल में,
मेरे संग वे पल पल में।।

जन्मे हम मानव बनकर,
सुसंस्कृत बनाते उनके कर,
भय सताए हमे कदा,
मुट्‌ठी में वे लेते हर

वे सहभागी मेरे हर कल में,
मेरे संग वे पल पल में।

यदि कभी कटु वचन हो कहते,
नयन उन्हें हो निष्ठुर कहते,
इनसे जो अश्रु बहते,
उनका होता इस जल में
मेरे संग वे पल पल में।

यदि जीत हो तो उनकी है,
यदि हार हो तो मेरी,
यदि धृष्टता हो मेरी या,
समय की हेरा-फेरी,
वे नाविक जीवन की कल-कल में
मेरे संग वे पल पल में।

कभी उपवन हो जीवन मेरा,
स्वयं मधुप बन जाऊं,
कभी चुनु मई पीत-पराग,
कभी वहाँ मैं मंडराऊं,

निर्देशक, पुष्पों की शतदल में,
मेरे संग वे पल पल में।

—पीयूष पाण्डया

## 13. भारत में शिक्षकों का...

माँ-बाप से भी ऊँचा मान होता है।
भारत में शिक्षकों का सम्मान होता है।

प्यार से, डाँट से या कभी इनकार से।
शिष्यों के लिए शिक्षक वरदान होता है।

मिट्टी को हीरा सा कोहिनूर बनाना,
नींव का ईंटों में योगदान होता है।

ज्ञान का भण्डार इनके चरणों में यारों,
रोम-रोम इनसे प्रकाशमान होता है।

जीवन अंश 'मानव' चरणों में अर्पण,
आँख खोल देख, कृपानिधान होता है।

भारत में शिक्षकों का.........।।

—मानस खत्री

## 14. गुरू का महत्त्व

गुरू का महत्त्व कभी होगा न कम
भले कर लें कितनी भी उन्नति हम
वैसे तो है इंटरनेट पर हर प्रकार का ज्ञान
पर अच्छे बुरे की नहीं है उसे पहचान
नहीं है शब्द कैसे करूं धन्यवाद
बस चाहिए हर पल आप सबका आशीर्वाद
हूं जहां आज मैं उसमें है बड़ा योगदान
आप सबका जिन्होंने दिया मुझे इतना ज्ञान
आपने बनाया है मुझे इस योग्य
कि प्राप्त करूं मैं अपना लक्ष्य
दिया है हर समय आपने सहारा
जब भी लगा कि मैं हारा
पर मैं हूं कितना मतलबी
याद किया न मैंने आपको कभी
आज करता हूं दिल से आप सबका सम्मान
आप सबको है मेरा शत-शत प्रणाम

**"हैप्पी-टिचर्स डे"**

—रूचि चड्ढा

## 15. शत-शत प्रणाम

वह कौन सा है पद,
जिसे देता ये जहां सम्मान।

वह कौन सा है पद,
जो करता है देशों का निर्माण।

वह कौन सा है पद,
जो बनाता है इंसान को इंसान।

वह कौन सा है पद,
जिसे करते हैं सभी प्रणाम।

वह कौन सा है पद,
जिसकी छाया में मिलता ज्ञान।

वह कौन सा है पद,
जो कराये सही दिशा की पहचान।

गुरु है इस पद का नाम।
मेरा सभी गुरुजनों को शत-शत प्रणाम।

– हेम ज्योत्सना

●●

# Biography of an Inspiring Teacher

## Dr. Sarvepalli Radhakrishnan

1) *"A good teacher must know how to arouse the interest of the pupil in the field of study for which he is responsible. He must himself be a master in the field of study and be in touch with the latest developments in the subject, he must himself be a fellow traveler in the exciting pursuit of knowledge"*
*- Dr. S. Radhakrishnan.*

2) Dr. Sarvepalli Radhakrishnan was born on September 5, 1888 in a poor Telugu Niyogi Brahmin family at Tiruttani, Madras, Tamil Nadu. He died on April 17, 1975. He was the son of Sarvepalli Veeraswami and Sitamma. His father was a subordinate revenue official for a local landlord. He was married to Sivakamu and they had 5 daughters and a son, Sarvepalli Gopal.

3) He was an ace Indian theorist, academician, statesman and significant intellectual of relative religious conviction and ideas. Radhakrishnan had his early education at Gowdie School, Tiruvallur and then went to the Lutheran Mission School in Tirupati for his high school. He joined the Voorhee's College in Vellore later in 1906, he graduated from Madras Christian College with a Master's degree in Philosophy.

4) Radhakrishnan wrote his thesis for the M.A. degree on "The Ethics of the Vedanta and its Metaphysical Presuppositions". Most of his education was supported through scholarships.

5) In April 1909, he was appointed to the Department of Philosophy, at the Madras Presidency College. In 1918, Doctor Radha Krishnan was appointed as the Professor of Philosophy, in the University of Mysore.

6) He had written many articles like The Quest, Journal of Philosophy and the International Journal of Ethics. His first book was The Philosophy of Rabindranath Tagore. Radhakrishnan's second book, The Reign of Religion in Contemporary Philosophy was published in 1920.

7) Radhakrishnan's books and articles drew the attention of Ashutosh Mookerjee, Vice Chancellor of Calcutta University and so designated him to the prestigious George V Professor of Philosophy at the Calcutta University. In 1921, he was appointed as a Professor to King George V Chair of Mental and Moral Science in the University of Calcutta.

8) In June 1926, he represented the University of Calcutta at the Congress of the Universities of the British Empire. In September 1926, Dr. Radhakrishnan represented the International Congress of Philosophy at the Harvard University.

9) In 1929, he was invited to take the post vacated by Principal J. Estin Carpenter, in Manchester College, Oxford.

10) In 1929 he was invited to deliver the Hibbert Lecture on the ideals of life at Harris Manchester College, Oxford which was afterwards printed in book form as An Idealist View of Life. In this book he made an influential case for the significance of instinctive thoughts as contrasting to merely academic forms of thinking.

11) He is recognized for his comments on the Prasthana Trayi explicitly, the Bhagavadgita, the Upanishads and the Brahma Sutra. He also updated himself with Buddhist and Jain beliefs and thoughts of Western thinkers such as Plato, Plotinus, Kant, Bradley, and Bergson.

12) He was knighted by the British government in the year 1931. In April 1932 he was honour by the Governor-General of India, the Earl of Willingdon award however he preferred using his academic title of 'Doctor' throughout his life. He was the Vice-Chancellor of Andhra University from 1931 to 1936. He was nominated for the Nobel Prize for literature for five consecutive years from 1933-1937.

13) From 1936-39, he served as the Spalding Professor of Eastern Religions and Ethics at Oxford University. In 1939, he was elected Fellow of the British Academy. In 1939 Pt. Madan Mohan Malaviya invited him to succeed him as the Vice-Chancellor of Banaras Hindu University (BHU). He served as its Vice-Chancellor till January 1948.

14) After our independence he was the leader of the Indian delegation to UNESCO during 1946-52 and was India's Ambassador to the Soviet Union from 1949 to 1952. He was also elected to the Constituent Assembly of India.

15) In 1948 Dr. Radhakrishnan was appealed to Chair the University Education Commission. He served as the Ambassador of India to U.S.S.R. during 1949-

52. Doctor Radha Krishnan was also a member of the Constituent Assembly of India.

16) Dr. Radhakrishnan was the Vice-President of India from 1952 to 1962 and the President, General Conference of UNESCO, from 1952 to 1954. He was honored with Bharat Ratna in 1954. He received the Peace Prize of the German Book Trade in 1961. In 1975, he received the Templeton Prize. He donated the entire amount of the Templeton Prize to Oxford University.

17) He held the office of the Chancellor, University of Delhi, from 1953-62. In May 1962, Dr. Radhakrishnan became the second President of India in 1962, a post he served till May 1967. When he became President, a few of his students and friends appealed him to permit them to commemorate his birthday, 5 September. He replied, "As an alternative of celebrating my birthday, it would be my proud privilege if 5 September is observed as Teachers' Day." Hence his birthday is celebrated as Teachers' Day in India.

18) He also won the Order of Merit award in 1963. Along with Ghanshyam Das Birla and some other social workers in the pre-independence era, Radhakrishnan formed the Krishnarpan Charity Trust.

19) During his tenure he faced enormous challenges like Indo-China war of 1962 during which he said to the nation, ""Owing to the difficult terrain and numerical superiority of the Chinese, we suffered military reverses. These have opened our eyes to the realities of the situation. We are now aware of our inadequacies and are alive to the needs of the present and the demands of the future. The country has developed a new purpose, a new will" and Indo-Pakistan war in 1965. As a President he facilitated India all the way through those difficult years securely. Dr Radhakrishnan in his broadcast to the nation on September 25, 1965 said, "Pakistan assumed that India was too weak or too afraid or too proud to fight. India, though naturally disinclined to take to arms felt the necessity to defend herself when attacked. Pakistan also assumed that communal disturbances would occur in the country and in the resulting chaos she could have her way. Her miscalculations must have come to her as a rude shock."

20) At the age of 79, Dr. Radhakrishnan returned to Madras in May 1967 where he spent his last years contentedly at his residence "Girija" in Mylapore, Madras. Pandit Jawaharlal Nehru said about Dr. Radhakrishnan: "He has served his country in many capacities. But above all, he is a great Teacher from whom all of us have learnt much and will continue to learn. It is India's peculiar privilege to have a great philosopher, a great educationist and a great humanist as her President. That in itself shows the kind of men we honour and respect."

●●

# Conclusion

guru brahma gurur vishnu
guru devo maheshwaraha
guru saakshat para brahma
tasmai sri-gurave namaha

गुरुर्ब्रह्मा गुरुर्विष्णुः गुरुर्देवो महेश्वरः।
गुरुरेव परंब्रह्म तस्मै श्रीगुरवे नमः।।

This means that guru is verily the representative of Brahma, Vishnu and Shiva. He creates, sustains knowledge and destroys the weeds of ignorance. I salute such a guru.

Many argue that the guru and shishya relationship we saw in the ancient India has lost all the sensation and teachers are no longer placed on a high pedestal in the society. It also means that teachers are no longer considered next to god in our country and that many people takes up teaching as their profession because they don't find any other suitable job.

However; I believe that even today teaching is considered as one of the noblest professions. The teacher sets the right foundation for any child on which their career and future depends. From my survey I have conducted on 50 teachers I found that in addition to academic qualifications teaching requires few other attributes like good communication skills, panache for interaction with the students (even their parents), good subject knowledge, exciting the interest among students and constantly nurturing them to meet their expectations as well as expectations of the highly competitive world are the five important requisites for any good teacher.

On the other hand, they also added that patience, self-confidence, determination, mutual understanding and devotion are the essential qualities for any successful teacher since they not only help students in shaping their careers but also in building the student's all round development. However, most of the teachers believe that if the university/ institute want to attract more efficient teachers, then they must lay emphasis on providing higher salaries so that the teachers are not compelled to teach in any private coaching or tuition classes.

We as teachers, through our dedication and devotion have to break the myths of people and find out different creative and innovative ways to polish the skills and competencies of our future generation. Carl Jung once said that one looks back with appreciation to the brilliant teachers, but with gratitude to those who touched our human feelings. The curriculum is so much necessary raw material, but warmth is the vital element for the growing plant and for the soul of the child. This will help us to be really excellent teachers rather than being just mediocre. Well, I wish you all the very best for a satisfying career.

●●

# Student Feedback Form For Teachers

As an institute we value your suggestions and feedback. So please be unbiased and rate the teacher on the below mentioned criteria, so that we can effectively meet your future needs and aspirations.

Student's name:- ________________________

Class:- ________________________

Teacher's name:- ________________________

Subject:- ________________________

| | | Excellent | Good | Average | Needs improvement | V. Poor |
|---|---|---|---|---|---|---|
| 1. | Punctuality | | | | | |
| 2. | Authenticity | | | | | |
| 3. | Availability | | | | | |
| 4. | Discipline | | | | | |
| 5. | Time management | | | | | |
| 6. | Explanation skill | | | | | |
| 7. | Subject knowledge | | | | | |
| 8. | Technique of teaching | | | | | |
| 9. | Nature | | | | | |
| 10. | Professionalism | | | | | |
| 11. | Difficulty solving approach | | | | | |

| 12. | Confidence | | | | | |
|---|---|---|---|---|---|---|
| 13. | Communication skill | | | | | |
| 14. | Ability to motivate | | | | | |
| 15. | Completion of syllabus | | | | | |
| 16. | Enthusiasm | | | | | |
| 17. | Fairness in evaluation | | | | | |
| 18. | Friendliness | | | | | |
| 19. | Creativity | | | | | |
| 20. | Flexibility | | | | | |
| 21. | Overall efficiency | | | | | |

Any other suggestions:-________________________________________

__________________________________________________________

__________________________________________________________

Describe any 2 strengths and weaknesses of the teacher:-

Strengths:-______________________________________________

__________________________________________________________

__________________________________________________________

Weaknesses:-_____________________________________________

__________________________________________________________

__________________________________________________________

# Student Feedback Form
# For Institute

As an institute we value your suggestions and feedback. So please be unbiased and rate the institute on the below mentioned criteria so that we can effectively meet your future needs and aspirations.

Student's name:- ______________________

Class:- ______________________

| | | Excellent | Good | Average | Needs improvement | V. Poor |
|---|---|---|---|---|---|---|
| 1. | Curriculum design | | | | | |
| 2. | Teachers and teaching technique | | | | | |
| 3. | Use of technological aid | | | | | |
| 4. | Lab facility | | | | | |
| 5. | Transport facility | | | | | |
| 6. | Internet facility | | | | | |
| 7. | Library facility | | | | | |
| 8. | Canteen facility | | | | | |
| 9. | Time schedule | | | | | |
| 10. | Co-curricular activities | | | | | |
| 11. | Extracurricular activities | | | | | |
| 12. | Examination pattern | | | | | |

| 13. | Results and assessment | | | | | |
|---|---|---|---|---|---|---|
| 14. | Event celebrations | | | | | |
| 15. | Attendance system | | | | | |
| 16. | Integrity and honesty | | | | | |
| 17. | Code of conduct | | | | | |
| 18. | Hostel facility (optional) | | | | | |
| 19. | Overall efficiency | | | | | |

In this academic session how was your overall experience with the institute:- ____

________________________________________________

________________________________________________

________________________________________________

Any other suggestions/ feedback:-________________________

________________________________________________

________________________________________________

# Teacher Feedback Form For Students

Teacher's name:- ______________________

Class:- ______________________

Student's name:- ______________________

Subject taught:- ______________________

Signature:- ______________________

Date:- ______________________

| | | Excellent | Good | Average | Needs improvement | V. Poor |
|---|---|---|---|---|---|---|
| 1. | Academic prospective | | | | | |
| 2. | Academic attainment | | | | | |
| 3. | Self motivation | | | | | |
| 4. | Interest in studies | | | | | |
| 5. | Team player | | | | | |
| 6. | Time management skills | | | | | |
| 7. | Stress management skills | | | | | |
| 8. | Communication skills | | | | | |
| 9. | Participation in extra-curricular activities | | | | | |
| 10. | Participation in co-curricular activities | | | | | |
| 11. | Creativity | | | | | |
| 12. | Self-confidence | | | | | |
| 13. | Sense of humour | | | | | |

| | | | | | | |
|---|---|---|---|---|---|---|
| 14. | Acceptance of responsibility | | | | | |
| 15. | Leadership skills | | | | | |
| 16. | Respect for elders | | | | | |
| 17. | Communication with other students | | | | | |
| 18. | Problem solving ability | | | | | |
| 19. | Following rules of institute | | | | | |
| 20. | Attendance and punctuality | | | | | |
| 21. | Co-operation | | | | | |
| 22. | General attitude | | | | | |
| 23. | Hygiene practices | | | | | |

Describe any 2 strengths and weaknesses of the student:-

Strengths:-________________________________________

________________________________________________

________________________________________________

Weaknesses:-______________________________________

________________________________________________

________________________________________________

Any other suggestions/ feedback:-__________________________

________________________________________________

________________________________________________

# Institute Feedback Form For Teachers

Principal's name:- ______________________

Teacher's name:- ______________________

Class:- ______________________

Subjects taught:- ______________________

Signature of the Principal:- ______________________

Date:- ______________________

| | | Excellent | Good | Average | Needs improvement | V. Poor |
|---|---|---|---|---|---|---|
| 1. | Regularity | | | | | |
| 2. | Dependability | | | | | |
| 3. | Accessibility | | | | | |
| 4. | Obedience | | | | | |
| 5. | Time management skills | | | | | |
| 6. | Rationalization skill | | | | | |
| 7. | Subject acquaintance | | | | | |
| 8. | Modus operandi of instruction | | | | | |

| | | | | | | |
|---|---|---|---|---|---|---|
| 9. | Temperament | | | | | |
| 10. | Professionalism | | | | | |
| 11. | Simplicity in answering queries | | | | | |
| 12. | Self-reliance | | | | | |
| 13. | Communication proficiency | | | | | |
| 14. | Capability to encourage | | | | | |
| 15. | Timely completion of syllabus | | | | | |
| 16. | Keenness | | | | | |
| 17. | Evenhandedness in assessment and appraisal | | | | | |
| 18. | Sociability | | | | | |
| 19. | Personal Vision | | | | | |
| 20. | Flexibility | | | | | |
| 21. | General competence | | | | | |
| | | | | | | |

In this academic session how was his/her overall performance in the institute:-

______________________________________________

______________________________________________

______________________________________________

Any other suggestions/ feedback:-______________________________

______________________________________________

______________________________________________

Describe any 2 strengths and weaknesses of the teacher:-

Strengths:-______________________________________

______________________________________________

______________________________________________

Weaknesses:-____________________________________

______________________________________________

______________________________________________

# Teacher Feedback Form For Institute

- Institute's name:- ______________________
- Teacher's name:- ______________________
- Class:- ______________________
  Subjects taught:- ______________________
- Signature of the teacher:- ______________________
- Date:- ______________________

| | | Excellent | Good | Average | Needs improvement | V. Poor |
|---|---|---|---|---|---|---|
| 1. | Syllabus design | | | | | |
| 2. | Vision and mission | | | | | |
| 3. | Availability of technological aid | | | | | |
| 4. | Ethical and moral values | | | | | |
| 5. | Lab facility | | | | | |
| 6. | Opportunity for career growth | | | | | |
| 7. | Transport facility | | | | | |
| 8. | Internet facility | | | | | |
| 9. | Congenial work environment | | | | | |
| 10. | Library facility | | | | | |
| 11. | Willingness to take risk | | | | | |
| 12. | Canteen facility | | | | | |

| | | | | | | |
|---|---|---|---|---|---|---|
| 13. | Time schedule | | | | | |
| 14. | Flexibility to adopt changes | | | | | |
| 15. | Co-curricular activities | | | | | |
| 16. | Extracurricular activities | | | | | |
| 17. | Examination pattern | | | | | |
| 18. | Remuneration/ monetary benefits | | | | | |
| 19. | Non-monetary benefits | | | | | |
| 20. | Fair recognition and reward policy | | | | | |
| 21. | Results and assessment guidance | | | | | |
| 22. | Event celebrations | | | | | |
| 23. | Ability to recognize opportunities | | | | | |
| 24. | Attendance system | | | | | |
| 25. | Listening skills | | | | | |
| 26. | Integrity and honesty | | | | | |
| 27. | Code of conduct | | | | | |
| 28. | Hostel facility (optional) | | | | | |
| 29. | Overall efficiency | | | | | |

Any other suggestions/ feedbacks:-______________________________________

______________________________________________________________

________________________________________________________

# Peers Feedback Form For Teachers

Colleague's name:- ____________________

Teacher's name:- ____________________

Class:- ____________________

Signature of the Colleague:- ____________________

Date:- ____________________

| | | Always | Often | Sometimes | Rarely | Never |
|---|---|---|---|---|---|---|
| 1. | Participation in institutes activities | | | | | |
| 2. | Punctuality | | | | | |
| 3. | Attending meetings | | | | | |
| 4. | Comes prepared for any meeting/ conferences | | | | | |
| 5. | Encouraging others | | | | | |
| 6. | Team player | | | | | |
| 7. | Sets mutual goals | | | | | |
| 8. | Gives positive comments | | | | | |
| 9. | Appreciates others | | | | | |
| 10. | Promote conviction and sincerity | | | | | |
| 11. | Respect others ideas/ views | | | | | |
| 12. | Encourages harmony and discussion | | | | | |
| 13. | Is proactive | | | | | |
| 14. | Promotes positive work environment | | | | | |
| 15. | Stress management | | | | | |

| | | | | | | |
|---|---|---|---|---|---|---|
| 16. | Motivates others to deal with stress | | | | | |
| 17. | Manages conflicts | | | | | |
| 18. | Shows initiative | | | | | |
| 19. | Works for the best | | | | | |
| 20. | Indulges in continuous learning process | | | | | |
| 21. | Is focused and positive | | | | | |
| 22. | Demonstrates leadership qualities | | | | | |
| 23. | Overall competence | | | | | |

If you have given low rating to your peer, please justify the reason for the same:

______________________________________________________________

______________________________________________________________

In this academic session how was his/her overall performance in the institute:- ____

______________________________________________________________

______________________________________________________________

Any other suggestions/ feedback:- ______________________________

______________________________________________________________

Describe any 2 strengths and weaknesses:-

Strengths:- ____________________________________________________

______________________________________________________________

Weaknesses:- __________________________________________________

______________________________________________________________

# Parent Feedback Form
# For Teacher

As an institute we value your suggestions and feedback as a good rapport between parents and teachers fosters communal trust and strong liaison. So please be unbiased and rate the teacher on the below mentioned criteria's so that we can effectively meet your child's future needs and aspirations.

Parent's name:- ____________________

Student's name:- ____________________

Teacher's name:- ____________________

Class:- ____________________

Subject taught:- ____________________

Signature of the parent:- ____________________

Date:- ____________________

| | | Excellent | Good | Average | Needs improvement | V. Poor |
|---|---|---|---|---|---|---|
| 1. | Regularity | | | | | |
| 2. | Dependability | | | | | |
| 3. | Availability | | | | | |
| 4. | Teaching experience | | | | | |
| 5. | Time management skills | | | | | |
| 6. | Explanation skill | | | | | |
| 7. | Subject knowledge | | | | | |
| 8. | Method of teaching | | | | | |
| 9. | Nature | | | | | |

| | | | | | | |
|---|---|---|---|---|---|---|
| 10. | Professionalism | | | | | |
| 11. | Difficulty solving approach | | | | | |
| 12. | Self-confidence | | | | | |
| 13. | Communication expertise | | | | | |
| 14. | Ability to motivate students | | | | | |
| 15. | Timely completion of syllabus | | | | | |
| 16. | Practice and revision | | | | | |
| 17. | Enthusiasm | | | | | |
| 18. | Attention to weak students | | | | | |
| 19. | Evenhandedness in assessment | | | | | |
| 20. | Affability/Friendliness | | | | | |
| 21. | Ingenuity | | | | | |
| 22. | Flexibility | | | | | |
| 23. | Sharing industry/ practical knowledge | | | | | |
| 24. | Sense of commitment | | | | | |
| 25. | Overall efficiency | | | | | |

If you have given low rating to the teacher, please justify the reason for the same:

______________________________________________

______________________________________________

______________________________________________

_______________________________________________

In this academic session how was your child's overall performance in the institute:-

_______________________________________________

_______________________________________________

Any other suggestions/ feedback:-_______________________________

_______________________________________________

_______________________________________________

Describe the teacher's any 2 strengths and weaknesses:-

Strengths:-_______________________________________

_______________________________________________

_______________________________________________

Weaknesses:-_____________________________________

_______________________________________________

_______________________________________________

# Parent Feedback Form
# For Institute

As an institute we value your suggestions and feedback. So please be unbiased and rate the institute on the below mentioned criteria so that we can effectively meet your future needs and aspirations.

Institute's name:- ______________________________

Parent's name:- ______________________________

Student's name:- ______________________________

Class:- ______________________________

Signature of the parent:- ______________________________

Date:- ______________________________

| | | Excellent | Good | Average | Needs improvement | V. Poor |
|---|---|---|---|---|---|---|
| 1. | Curriculum design | | | | | |
| 2. | Teachers and teaching technique | | | | | |
| 3. | Use of technological aid | | | | | |
| 4. | Lab facility | | | | | |
| 5. | Transport facility | | | | | |
| 6. | Internet facility | | | | | |
| 7. | Library facility | | | | | |
| 8. | Canteen facility | | | | | |
| 9. | Time schedule | | | | | |
| 10. | Co-curricular activities | | | | | |
| 11. | Extracurricular activities | | | | | |

| | | | | | | |
|---|---|---|---|---|---|---|
| 12. | Examination pattern | | | | | |
| 13. | Results and assessment | | | | | |
| 14. | Event celebrations | | | | | |
| 15. | Attendance system | | | | | |
| 16. | Integrity and honesty | | | | | |
| 17. | Code of conduct | | | | | |
| 18. | Hostel facility (optional) | | | | | |
| 19. | Infrastructure | | | | | |
| 20. | Professionalism | | | | | |
| 21. | Attention to weak students | | | | | |
| 22. | Industry/ practical exposure | | | | | |
| 23. | Enhancement of communication skills | | | | | |
| 24. | Sense of commitment | | | | | |
| 25. | Placement facility (optional) | | | | | |
| 26. | Overall efficiency | | | | | |

If you have given low rating to the institute, please justify the reason for the same:

________________________________________

________________________________________

________________________________________

In this academic session how was your child's overall experience with the institute:-

________________________________________________________________________

________________________________________________________________________

________________________________________________________________________

Any other suggestions/ feedback-________________________________________

________________________________________________________________________

________________________________________________________________________